MALAGA COSTA DEL SOL TRAVEL GUIDE

2024 Edition

Malaga Unveiled: Unveiling the Best Beaches, Historic Treasures, and Culinary Delights of Andalusia's Coastal Paradise

By

Williams Carter

Copyright©2023 Williams Carter

All Right Reserved

TABLE OF CONTENT

IMPORTANT NOTE BEFORE READING

INTRODUCTION

Embracing the Allure of Malaga and the Costa del Sol
A Brief Overview of the Region's History and Culture

CHAPTER ONE

GETTING READY FOR YOUR JOURNEY
1.1 Planning Your Trip: When to Go and What to Pack
1.2 Navigating Transportation: Airports, Trains, and Local Travel Tips
1.2.1 Airports:
1.2.2 Trains:
1.2.3 Buses and Trams:
1.2.4 Rental Cars:
1.2.5 Biking and Walking:
1.2.6 Taxis and Ride-Sharing:
1.3 Recommended Local Apps For Booking Transport

CHAPTER TWO

MALAGA: PICASSO'S HOMETOWN AND BEYOND
2.1 Unveiling the Rich Heritage of Malaga
2.2 Exploring the Picasso Museum and Tracing the Artist's Roots
2.3 Roaming the Alcazaba Fortress and Gibralfaro Castle
2.4 Strolling Through the Lively Streets of Malaga's Old Town

CHAPTER THREE

SUN-KISSED BEACHES AND COASTAL DELIGHTS

3.1 DISCOVERING THE BEST BEACHES ALONG THE COSTA DEL SOL

3.1.1 Playa de la Malagueta:

3.1.2 Playa de la Misericordia:

3.2 ENGAGING IN WATER SPORTS AND ACTIVITIES FOR THRILL-SEEKERS

3.2.1 Waterskiing and Wakeboarding:

3.2.2 Kite Surfing and Wind Surfing:

3.3 RELAXING IN CHARMING COASTAL VILLAGES: NERJA, MARBELLA, AND BEYOND

3.3.1 Nerja:

3.3.2 Marbella:

3.3.3 Estepona:

3.3.4 Fuengirola:

3.3.5 Manilva and Casares:

CHAPTER FOUR

CULTURAL IMMERSION: FLAMENCO, FESTIVALS, AND GASTRONOMY

4.1 EXPERIENCING THE PASSIONATE ART OF FLAMENCO DANCING

4.2 JOINING FESTIVALS AND CELEBRATIONS: SEMANA SANTA AND FERIA DE MALAGA

4.3 SAVORING ANDALUSIAN CUISINE: TAPAS, SEAFOOD, AND TRADITIONAL DISHES

4.3.1 Recommended Top Restaurants and Their Locations:

4.3.2 Recommended Top Nightclubs and Bars and Their Locations:

CHAPTER FIVE

ARCHITECTURAL WONDERS: MOORISH SPLENDORS AND MODERN MARVELS

5.1 ADMIRING THE LEGACY OF MOORISH ARCHITECTURE: ALHAMBRA AND NASRID PALACES

5.2 Exploring Malaga's Modern Architectural Gems: Pompidou Center and More

CHAPTER SIX

NATURAL ESCAPES: MOUNTAINS, CAVES, AND NATIONAL PARKS
6.1 Venturing into the Sierra de las Nieves Natural Park
6.2 Unearthing the Wonders of Nerja's Caves and Cliffs
6.3 Hiking the Majestic Mountains and Enjoying Breathtaking Views

CHAPTER SEVEN

LEISURE AND ENTERTAINMENT
7.1 Embracing Nightlife in Malaga and Coastal Hotspots
7.2 Shopping, Markets, and Local Handicrafts: Where to Find the Best Souvenirs
7.3 Enjoying Family-Friendly Activities and Amusement Parks

CHAPTER EIGHT

ACCOMMODATION OPTION
8.1 Luxury Resorts and Villas
8.1.1 Recommended Top Luxury Resorts And Villas With Their Locations
8.2 Boutique Hotels and Charming Inns
8.2.1 Recommended Top Boutique Hotels and Charming Inns With Their Locations
8.3 Cozy Beachfront B&Bs
8.3.1 Recommended Top Cozy Beachfront B&Bs With Their Locations
8.4 Hostels and Guest Houses
8.4.1 Recommended Top Hostels and Guest Houses With Their Locations

8.5 BEST NEIGHBORHOODS TO STAY
8.6 LOCAL APPS FOR BOOKING ACCOMMODATION

CHAPTER NINE

DAY TRIPS AND BEYOND
9.1 EXPLORING RONDA: A TOWN ON THE EDGE OF THE CLIFF
9.2 JOURNEYING TO GRANADA: ALHAMBRA AND ALBAICÍN DISTRICT
9.3 VENTURING INTO THE HISTORIC CITY OF CORDOBA

CHAPTER TEN

PRACTICAL INFORMATION AND RESOURCES
10.1 USEFUL TRAVEL TIPS FOR A SMOOTH VISIT
10.2 LANGUAGE, CURRENCY, AND COMMUNICATION ESSENTIALS

CONCLUSION

REFLECTING ON YOUR MALAGA AND COSTA DEL SOL ADVENTURE
FOND MEMORIES AND INSPIRATIONS FOR FUTURE JOURNEYS

IMPORTANT NOTE BEFORE READING

You might find a special trip experience in these pages.

The purpose of this Malaga and Costa del Sol travel guide is to inspire your creativity, imagination, and sense of adventure. Since we think that the beauty of every discovery should be experienced firsthand, free from visual filter and prejudices, you won't find any pictures here. Every monument, every location, and every secret nook are waiting for you when you get there, eager to surprise and amaze you. Why should we ruin the wonder and excitement of the initial impression? Prepare to set off on a voyage where your imagination will serve as both your single mode of transportation and your personal tour guide. Keep in mind that your own creations are the most attractive.

This book lacks a map and photographs, in contrast to many other manuals. Why? Because in our opinion the best discoveries are made when a person gets lost, lets themselves go with the flow of the environment, and embraces the ambiguity of the road.

Be cautious, trust your gut, and expect the unexpected. In a world without maps, where roads are made with each step you take, the magic of the voyage starts now.

INTRODUCTION

Embracing the Allure of Malaga and the Costa del Sol

Nestled harmoniously along the sun-drenched southern coast of Spain, the enchanting city of Malaga and its neighboring Costa del Sol region cast a spell that is both irresistible and magnetic, luring travelers from every corner of the world. This chapter stands as your welcoming gateway, inviting you to step into the heart of this captivating destination, unraveling its hidden treasures and understanding the intricate tapestry of its identity – a tapestry woven with threads of picturesque landscapes and vibrant culture.

The very air you breathe seems imbued with a sense of adventure and discovery as you set foot on the shores of this coastal haven. The glistening expanse of the Mediterranean Sea stretches out before you, its waves whispering tales of seafarers and explorers who once charted these waters. The golden sun, a benevolent guardian, embraces the land with its warm rays, bestowing a sense of comfort and vitality upon all who bask in its radiance. And as you traverse the charming streets, the gentle breeze carries the delicate fragrance of blooming bougainvillea, painting the pathways with a spectrum of colors that harmonize with the vivacity of the surroundings.

The allure of Malaga and the Costa del Sol is a symphony of experiences, a composition that resonates deeply within the recesses of your soul. It's in the laughter of locals as they gather at lively tapas bars, sharing stories and savoring culinary delights. It's in the rhythm of flamenco dancers' feet, pounding out stories of passion, heartache, and triumph. It's in the history-rich walls of the Alcazaba fortress, echoing with whispers of civilizations that once thrived within its protective embrace. It's in the contemporary beats of the Pompidou Center, a testament to the city's modern artistic spirit.

As you embark on your journey through this enchanting tapestry, every step is an opportunity to immerse yourself in the tapestry's intricate details. Discover the artistry of Picasso, who was born here and left an indelible mark on the city's cultural legacy. Traverse the bustling markets where the mingling of languages and scents forms a vibrant cultural mosaic. Feel the pulse of life in the Old Town, where historic architecture and modern cafes coexist in harmony.

The allure of Malaga and the Costa del Sol transcends the tangible, creating a mosaic of memories that will linger long after you've left its shores. It's the taste of salt on your lips as you dip into the sea, the echo of laughter in beachside chiringuitos, and the warmth of the locals' hospitality that warms your heart. It's an enchantment that will forever be etched in your memory, beckoning you to return and rediscover the symphony of experiences that await in this captivating corner of the world.

A Brief Overview of the Region's History and Culture

Truly appreciating the present entails embarking on a journey that peels back the layers of time, revealing the intricate tapestry of history and culture that has meticulously woven the fabric of Malaga and the Costa del Sol. This chapter is your time machine, transporting you through the annals of ages, from the dawn of ancient civilizations to the contemporary pulse of modern times. With each step, you'll gain insights into the diverse influences that have contributed to the region's unparalleled and captivating identity.

The echoes of centuries past resonate through the streets and alleyways, whispering stories of the civilizations that once called this land home. The Phoenician and Roman settlements, now but remnants, stand as silent witnesses to the ebbs and flows of time. As you explore, the architectural marvels of Moorish rule cast a spell, their intricate designs and elegant forms carrying you back to an era of artistic grandeur and cultural exchange.

The historical narrative of Malaga and the Costa del Sol is a rich tapestry woven with threads of conquest and liberation, each thread a unique story that has shaped the destiny of this region. From the triumphant stories of liberation to the struggles of conquest, the very soil seems imbued with the essence of the past.

Amid this historical tableau, the figure of Pablo Picasso emerges, a luminary whose presence is deeply interwoven with the city's essence. Born in Malaga, his artistic genius has left an indelible mark on the cultural landscape. Picasso's influence can be felt in every corner, from the vibrant art scene to the Picasso Museum that proudly houses a diverse collection of his masterpieces.

As you journey through this chapter, you'll traverse not only geographical landscapes but also the landscapes of time. The layers of history unfold before you, revealing the mosaic of influences that have contributed to the region's unique identity. With every page turned, you'll dive deeper into the cultural mosaic that defines Malaga and the Costa del Sol.

By understanding the past, you'll be better equipped to appreciate the present and anticipate the future. The diverse influences that have converged on this land have created a vibrant and multifaceted culture, setting the stage for a journey of exploration that transcends time itself. As you absorb the tales of triumph, the echoes of battles, and the whispers of artistic genius, you'll find yourself inextricably linked to the essence of the region's past and present. This chapter is your guide, inviting you to explore with open eyes and a heart eager to embrace the richness of Malaga's history and culture.

CHAPTER ONE

GETTING READY FOR YOUR JOURNEY

1.1 Planning Your Trip: When to Go and What to Pack

When embarking on a journey to Malaga and the Costa del Sol, strategic planning is key to making the most of your experience. The region's Mediterranean climate offers a generally pleasant environment throughout the year, but certain seasons may align better with your preferences and interests.

When to Go:

Spring (March to May): A Season of Delightful Awakening

Spring emerges as a truly enchanting time to venture into the heart of Malaga and the Costa del Sol. With the transition from the coolness of winter to the gentle warmth of spring, the region bursts forth in a riot of colors and scents. March ushers in the season, offering travelers a respite from the chilly months that preceded it. The weather begins to shed its winter coat, revealing a mild and inviting embrace that is perfect for exploration.

One of the most captivating aspects of spring in Malaga and the Costa del Sol is the exquisite floral display. As temperatures climb and the sun regains its strength, flowers of all kinds burst into bloom, painting the landscapes with vibrant hues. The almond blossoms are among the first to adorn the countryside, creating a dreamy and almost surreal backdrop. Streets, parks, and gardens are adorned with a myriad of flowers, each contributing to the region's charming allure.

Beyond the visual spectacle, spring is also a time when the spirit of festivity envelopes the region. Traditional festivals and events come to life, celebrating the season's revival and the rich cultural heritage of the area. Streets echo with music, laughter, and vibrant processions as locals and visitors alike take part in the festivities. Semana Santa, the Holy Week, takes center stage during spring, presenting an awe-inspiring spectacle of religious devotion and intricate processions.

The advantage of visiting during spring extends beyond the aesthetic and cultural. As the winter crowds recede, the tourist influx diminishes, leaving behind a quieter, more serene atmosphere. This means that the popular attractions and landmarks can be savored with a sense of tranquility that is often elusive during the bustling summer months. The weather, with its gentle warmth and relatively low rainfall, sets the stage for outdoor exploration, whether it's wandering through historic streets, hiking in the surrounding hills, or enjoying leisurely strolls along the coastline.

Summer (June to August): The Sizzle of High Season

With the arrival of June, the Costa del Sol transforms into a sun-soaked paradise that beckons travelers from all corners of the globe. Summer is undoubtedly the peak tourist season, marked by an explosion of vitality and energy. This is the time when beach lovers, sun seekers, and families converge upon the coast to indulge in the pleasures of the Mediterranean.

The weather during the summer months is characterized by its ardent embrace. The sun reigns supreme, casting its golden glow over sandy shores and inviting azure waters. Days are long and nights are balmy, creating an ambiance that is synonymous with relaxation and outdoor revelry. It's the ideal climate for beachgoers, as temperatures often soar, enticing visitors to bask in the sun, swim in the sparkling sea, and partake in a variety of water sports.

The coastal towns come alive during this period, bustling with life and brimming with activities. Street markets, open-air concerts, and beachside parties offer a dynamic and vibrant atmosphere. However, it's important to note that the popularity of the season also means larger crowds. Tourist hotspots can get quite congested, and accommodations and flights might require booking well in advance.

Fall (September to November): Autumn's Gentle Embrace

As the sun-tinged days of summer gradually wane, the Costa del Sol undergoes a serene transformation. The months of September to November usher in the quieter, mellower tones of autumn. This season presents a particularly appealing blend of warmth and tranquility, making it an excellent time to explore the region without the fervor of summer crowds.

The climate during early fall retains much of the summer's warmth, allowing for pleasant daytime excursions and coastal experiences. The sea, still bathed in the lingering heat, remains inviting for swimmers and water enthusiasts. This presents a unique opportunity to savor the Mediterranean waters without the bustling atmosphere of summer.

Cultural events and festivals continue to grace the calendar during the fall months, allowing travelers to engage with the local heritage in a more intimate setting. The grape harvest season, for instance, often brings about wine-related events, celebrating the rich viticultural traditions of the area.

Winter (December to February): A Tranquil Interlude

As winter takes hold in other parts of Europe, the Costa del Sol embraces a different kind of serenity. December to February offers a quieter and more introspective experience, ideal for those seeking respite from the more crowded seasons. While the weather remains milder than many other destinations in Europe, it's important to prepare for cooler temperatures, especially in the evenings.

The charm of winter lies in its unhurried pace. The bustling streets of summer and the festive ambiance of spring give way to a more contemplative ambiance. The beaches, though quieter, still offer tranquil spots to enjoy the crisp sea breeze. Historical sites and museums welcome visitors without the queues and commotion of peak seasons, allowing for a deeper connection with the cultural and artistic heritage of the region.

Moreover, the winter months offer an opportunity to embrace the local lifestyle, engaging with the everyday rhythms of Malaga and its surrounding towns. With fewer tourists around, interactions with locals take on a more personal and authentic character.

In conclusion, the four seasons of Malaga and the Costa del Sol each offer their own unique allure. Whether you're drawn to the exuberance of summer, the vivid blossoms of spring, the mellowness of fall, or the tranquility of winter, this region invites exploration and enchantment year-round.

What to Pack:

Packing Essentials for a Memorable Malaga and Costa del Sol Adventure

Preparing for your journey to Malaga and the Costa del Sol involves more than just anticipation—it requires thoughtful packing to ensure a comfortable and enjoyable experience. Whether you're basking in the summer sun, wandering the historic streets, or exploring cultural events, having the right items in your suitcase can greatly enhance your stay. Here's a guide to essential items you should consider including:

Light Clothing: Versatility and Comfort

No matter the season, lightweight and breathable clothing form the foundation of a pleasant stay in Malaga and the Costa del Sol. These essentials help you stay comfortable while you immerse yourself in the region's treasures. T-shirts, shorts, and casual dresses are excellent choices, allowing you to seamlessly transition from exploring historic sites to relaxing on the beach.

Swimsuits and Beach Attire: Embracing Coastal Delights

With the inviting Mediterranean Sea at your doorstep, packing swimsuits and beach attire is essential. Whether you're planning to dip your toes in the refreshing waters or fully immerse yourself in aquatic adventures, having proper swimwear ensures you're ready to embrace the coastal delights.

Sun Protection: Guarding Against the Mediterranean Sun

The radiant Mediterranean sun is a beloved aspect of the region, but it's crucial to protect yourself from its intensity. Sunscreen, wide-brimmed hats, and UV-blocking sunglasses are your allies in guarding against sunburn and ensuring you can revel in the outdoors without worry.

Layering Items: Preparing for Temperature Shifts

Even during the warmth of summer, evenings can bring cooler temperatures, especially near the coast. Including a light jacket or sweater in your packing list allows you to comfortably extend your explorations into the night, whether you're indulging in a seaside dinner or taking a leisurely stroll along the promenade.

Comfortable Walking Shoes: Navigating with Ease

Malaga and the Costa del Sol offer a treasure trove of historical sites, charming streets, and vibrant markets waiting to be explored on foot. Comfortable walking shoes are essential to ensure you can traverse cobbled alleys, sandy beaches, and picturesque town squares without discomfort.

Adapter and Chargers: Staying Connected

To stay connected and keep your devices powered up, remember to pack the appropriate power adapters and chargers. European power outlets are different from those in other parts of the world, so having the right adapters ensures your devices remain functional throughout your journey.

Local Guidebook: Enhancing Your Exploration

While you have a comprehensive guide at your disposal, carrying a compact local guidebook can be a valuable addition. These guides often provide on-the-go insights, hidden gems, and tips that further enrich your experience as you navigate the region.

As you embark on your adventure to Malaga and the Costa del Sol, packing these essentials ensures you're well-prepared to embrace the diverse charms of this captivating destination. From savoring the Mediterranean sun to exploring historical marvels, your packing choices play a crucial role in making your journey unforgettable.

1.2 Navigating Transportation: Airports, Trains, and Local Travel Tips

Getting to Malaga and navigating the Costa del Sol is relatively easy, thanks to its well-connected transportation network.

1.2.1 Airports:

Malaga-Costa del Sol Airport (AGP): Your Gateway to the Mediterranean Beauty

Malaga-Costa del Sol Airport (AGP) stands as the primary entry point to the captivating wonders of the Costa del Sol.

Serving as the region's main international airport, AGP plays a pivotal role in connecting travelers from around the world to the enchanting landscapes, rich history, and vibrant culture of Malaga and its surrounding coastal areas.

Seamless Connectivity to Major Cities: Your Travel Hub

Situated just a short distance from the heart of Malaga, AGP provides travelers with an efficient and convenient gateway to the entire Costa del Sol. Boasting a well-established infrastructure, the airport is exceptionally well-connected to major cities across Europe and beyond. This exceptional connectivity ensures that whether you're coming from London, Paris, Berlin, or other international hubs, you can easily access the treasures that await you in this sun-kissed Spanish paradise.

A Tapestry of Flights: Scheduled and Charter

AGP offers a diverse range of flight options, catering to various travel preferences and needs. From scheduled flights operated by major airlines to charter flights that provide flexibility and tailored travel experiences, the airport accommodates a plethora of flight choices. Whether you're a business traveler seeking efficiency or a leisure explorer in search of unique adventures, the airport's array of flight options allows you to craft your journey according to your desires.

The Arrival Experience: An Invitation to the Costa del Sol

Stepping off the plane at AGP, you're greeted by the warmth and hospitality that are emblematic of the region. The airport's modern facilities and efficient services ensure a seamless transition from the skies to the coastal landscapes that await you. As you traverse the terminals, you'll find an array of amenities, from shops offering local products to dining establishments where you can savor both traditional Spanish flavors and international cuisine.

Connecting with the Region: Beyond the Airport

AGP's strategic location in close proximity to Malaga and the Costa del Sol makes it a perfect starting point for your exploration. Convenient transportation options, including buses, taxis, and car rentals, allow you to seamlessly connect with your chosen destination. Whether you're embarking on a cultural journey through Malaga's historical streets, venturing to the charming towns nestled along the coast, or immersing yourself in the vibrant atmosphere of local festivals, AGP sets the stage for your captivating experience.

In conclusion, Malaga-Costa del Sol Airport (AGP) serves as the portal to the Mediterranean beauty that awaits you. Its extensive connectivity, welcoming facilities, and proximity to the region's treasures make it an integral part of your journey. Whether you're arriving to bask in the summer sun, indulge in cultural exploration, or savor the vibrant coastal lifestyle, AGP ensures your adventure begins with comfort and convenience, setting the tone for the unforgettable experiences that lie ahead in the heart of the Costa del Sol.

1.2.2 Trains:
Effortless Exploration with RENFE Trains: Unveiling Spain's High-Speed Connectivity

When it comes to seamless and picturesque travel between Malaga and other major Spanish cities, RENFE trains emerge as the embodiment of convenience, speed, and captivating landscapes. Operating under the flagship of Spain's national rail service, RENFE's high-speed AVE trains provide an exceptional mode of transportation that allows you to journey from Malaga to Madrid and beyond while reveling in the natural beauty of the Spanish countryside.

A Symphony of Speed and Comfort: High-Speed AVE Trains

The RENFE high-speed AVE trains epitomize efficiency, whisking travelers away at impressive speeds, ensuring they reach their destinations swiftly without compromising on comfort. These state-of-the-art trains redefine travel, offering luxurious seating, ample legroom, and a range of onboard amenities. As you glide along the tracks, you'll experience a sense of elegance and refinement that's second to none.

Connecting Malaga and Beyond: A Voyage of Discovery

The connection forged by the RENFE AVE trains between Malaga and major Spanish cities presents a doorway to explore the diverse facets of the nation. Notably, the route linking Malaga to Madrid is a prime example of this connectivity. The journey unfolds as a captivating voyage, taking you from the heart of Andalusia to the vibrant hub of Spain's capital. This expedition doesn't just bridge geographical distances—it also bridges cultural experiences, enabling you to immerse yourself in the distinct flavors and vibes of both regions.

Scenic Splendor: A Visual Feast

As the high-speed train glides through the Spanish landscape, travelers are treated to an ever-changing panorama of natural beauty. The journey is a visual feast, where rolling hills, sun-kissed vineyards, and charming villages create an enchanting tapestry outside your window. The RENFE AVE trains present a unique opportunity to savor the Spanish countryside from a privileged vantage point, making your travel experience not just about the destination, but also about the journey itself.

A Tapestry of Experiences: Beyond the Tracks

Beyond the seamless travel and captivating scenery, the RENFE AVE trains also provide you with precious moments of reflection and relaxation. It's a time to delve into that captivating novel you've been carrying, to gaze out the window and let your thoughts wander, or simply to enjoy a moment of reprieve from the fast-paced world.

Unlocking Exploration: Your Ticket to Unforgettable Journeys

In conclusion, the RENFE high-speed AVE trains are more than just a means of transportation; they are a gateway to exploration, adventure, and discovery. Whether you're embarking on a journey to Madrid, connecting to other Spanish cities, or savoring the scenic splendor that unfolds outside your window, RENFE AVE trains redefine your travel experience. From the moment you step onboard to the time you arrive at your destination, you're invited to be part of a narrative that seamlessly blends modern comfort with timeless beauty—a narrative that encapsulates the essence of Spain's remarkable landscapes and cultural diversity.

Local Travel Tips:

1.2.3 Buses and Trams:

In the heart of Malaga, a well-orchestrated transport network awaits to whisk you away on an adventure through the city's vibrant streets and nearby locales. This network, comprising efficient buses and convenient trams, forms the backbone of urban mobility, allowing you to effortlessly traverse the various facets of this captivating destination.

Embracing Urban Mobility: Efficient Bus Network

At the core of Malaga's transportation tapestry lies an extensive bus network that intricately weaves through the city's veins. This network, meticulously designed to cater to both residents and visitors, ensures that no corner of Malaga remains unexplored. Whether you're venturing to iconic landmarks, charming neighborhoods, or cultural hotspots, the buses are a reliable ally in your urban exploration.

The beauty of the bus system lies not just in its reach, but also in its frequency and connectivity. Buses, adorned with the vibrant hues of Malaga's urban landscape, grace the streets with regularity, minimizing wait times and maximizing your time for discovery. With routes that span from the bustling city center to the serene coastal stretches, you're invited to hop on board and partake in the rhythmic pulse of the city.

Trams: A Convenient Pathway

Complementing the bus network is Malaga's modern tram system, which offers an efficient and convenient way to navigate the urban expanse. The trams trace carefully planned routes, effortlessly connecting key areas within the city. As you step onto a tram, you're greeted by a sleek and contemporary mode of transport that seamlessly blends functionality with aesthetics.

The trams provide a vantage point from which to admire the urban beauty and architectural marvels of Malaga. Gliding along the tracks, you're treated to panoramic views of the city's blend of historic charm and modern vibrancy. Whether you're embarking on a sightseeing excursion or simply enjoying the journey, the trams offer an experience that transcends mere transportation.

Seamless Transitions: The Joy of Public Transport

One of the joys of utilizing public transport in Malaga is the seamless transitions it offers. Whether you're hopping off a bus to explore a historical monument or disembarking from a tram to delve into a cultural institution, the integration of these modes of transport makes your explorations fluid and effortless. Public transport not only facilitates efficient mobility but also enhances your immersion in the city's dynamic energy.

Unlocking the City's Treasures: Public Transport's Role

In the grand tapestry of Malaga's urban landscape, buses and trams are the threads that connect diverse elements, weaving them into a harmonious experience. They're not merely means of getting from point A to point B; they're gateways to the city's hidden corners, its vibrant neighborhoods, and its rich cultural offerings. As you embark on your journey, let the buses and trams be your companions, guiding you through a city that beckons with its allure and unfolds its treasures with each stop and start.

1.2.4 Rental Cars:

While the heart of Malaga beckons with its captivating sights and sounds, the allure of the surrounding countryside and coastal gems is equally irresistible. If you're harboring dreams of venturing beyond the city limits to uncover hidden villages, breathtaking viewpoints, and lesser-explored wonders, then renting a car opens up a world of possibilities.

Unveiling Hidden Treasures: Beyond City Limits

Renting a car in Malaga grants you the freedom to craft your own itinerary, weaving together a tapestry of experiences that resonates with your travel desires. Embarking on a road trip along the Costa del Sol or into the enchanting Andalusian countryside allows you to stumble upon places that may not be part of the typical tourist circuit. Secluded coves, charming white-washed villages, and panoramic landscapes await your discovery, and having a car at your disposal means you can explore them at your own pace.

Flexibility of Time: Your Journey, Your Schedule

One of the most significant advantages of renting a car is the liberation from the constraints of public transport schedules. You have the autonomy to set your own timeline, allowing you to linger in a picturesque spot, embrace a breathtaking viewpoint, or spontaneously stop at a roadside café that catches your eye. This control over your journey enhances the sense of adventure, as you navigate the roads with a sense of curiosity and anticipation.

Navigating Beyond the Beaten Path: Experiential Travel

With a rental car, you can delve into the heart of authenticity, delving into areas that may not be easily accessible via public transport. The winding roads that lead to lesser-known destinations invite you to connect with the local culture, engage with communities, and experience the unfiltered essence of the region. Whether it's savoring regional delicacies in a remote taverna or stumbling upon a traditional festival, your car becomes a vehicle for experiential travel that goes beyond the surface.

Challenges of Urban Parking: A Consideration

While a rental car empowers your exploration, it's essential to consider the practicalities, particularly when navigating city centers. Malaga, like many vibrant urban areas, poses challenges when it comes to parking. The narrow streets and limited parking spaces can prove to be daunting, especially in the historic quarters. However, the presence of parking garages and lots can offer a solution, ensuring your vehicle is safely stowed while you delve into the city's urban charm.

The Symphony of Travel Freedom

In the grand symphony of travel options, renting a car harmonizes the melody of spontaneity with the rhythm of exploration. It's an invitation to journey beyond the city's boundaries, to unveil the myriad treasures that await in the surrounding landscapes. With each turn of the wheel, you embrace the thrill of the unknown and the delight of discovery, all while maintaining the control and flexibility that amplifies the beauty of your travel experience.

1.2.5 Biking and Walking:

In the heart of Malaga and along its enchanting coastal stretches, a world of discovery unfolds for those who choose to traverse it on two feet or two wheels. The city's commitment to being bike and pedestrian-friendly forms the foundation for an immersive and intimate exploration of its charming landscapes, historical wonders, and the alluring Mediterranean ambiance.

Pedal Power: Cycling the Cultural Canvas

With its dedicated bike lanes and pathways, Malaga invites you to embrace the rhythm of the city on a bicycle. Renting a bike is not just a mode of transportation; it's a ticket to a unique perspective, allowing you to effortlessly glide through the streets, alleyways, and promenades that define the city's character. As you pedal, you're not merely a spectator but a participant in the daily life that unfolds around you.

Cycling presents a wonderful synergy of activity and discovery. You can embark on thematic journeys, tracing the city's history through its architectural gems or immersing yourself in its artistic pulse by exploring its galleries and creative hubs. Whether you're embarking on a solo exploration or joining guided biking tours, each rotation of the pedal propels you into an engaging narrative, unveiling layers of culture, art, and history.

Leisurely Strolls: Unraveling the Intricacies

If you're inclined towards unhurried exploration, Malaga's pedestrian-friendly character welcomes you with open arms. The city's walkable streets, plazas, and pathways invite you to take leisurely strolls that evoke a sense of timelessness. As you meander through the historic quarters, the aroma of local delicacies wafting from charming cafes, the rhythmic chatter of locals, and the sun-drenched architecture come together to create a symphony of sensory delights.

Strolling through Malaga's labyrinthine lanes allows you to engage with the details that might otherwise go unnoticed. Every turn presents an opportunity to stumble upon hidden courtyards, discover intricately adorned façades, and exchange smiles with passersby who embody the warmth of the Mediterranean spirit.

Immersive Connection: Pedal and Step into the Local Pulse

Renting a bike or embarking on leisurely strolls isn't just about exploration—it's about forging an immersive connection with the surroundings. You become attuned to the nuances of the city's character, engaging with its pace, its people, and its unique charm. Whether it's the feeling of the sea breeze as you cycle along the waterfront promenade or the sense of wonder as you pause to admire a centuries-old building, the experiences become etched in your memory as threads woven into the fabric of your journey.

A Journey by Pedal and Foot: A Different Perspective

In the tapestry of travel experiences, choosing to explore Malaga by bike or on foot is akin to embracing a different perspective—one that unfolds at a pace aligned with the heartbeat of the city. It's a chance to step away from the rush, to engage with your surroundings intimately, and to uncover the beauty that often escapes hurried eyes. Each pedal stroke and every step become an act of immersion, allowing you to capture not just photographs but also memories that resonate long after you've left the city's embrace.

1.2.6 Taxis and Ride-Sharing:

As you traverse the vibrant streets and avenues of Malaga, you'll find a spectrum of transportation options that cater to your convenience and comfort. Whether you're seeking a swift ride to your destination or an efficient way to explore the city's treasures, taxis and ride-sharing services stand ready to ensure you reach your desired stops seamlessly.

Taxis: Your On-Demand Chauffeurs

Malaga's bustling urban scene is punctuated by the ubiquitous presence of taxis, offering a reliable and accessible mode of transport for both locals and visitors. Taxis provide the ease of on-demand service, allowing you to simply flag one down or find them stationed at designated taxi ranks throughout the city. These modern vehicles, often adorned with a distinctive color, whisk you away to your chosen destinations with professionalism and efficiency.

Taxis offer not only speed but also a personal touch. As you sit back and journey through the streets, the friendly drivers are often more than willing to share insights about the city's highlights, recommend local eateries, or suggest hidden gems that might not be part of your original itinerary.

Ride-Sharing Services: Modern Convenience at Your Fingertips

The digital age has introduced a new dimension of convenience with the emergence of ride-sharing services. Companies such as Uber and similar platforms operate in the region, providing an innovative way to hail a ride using your smartphone. With a few taps, you can summon a ride to your location, track the driver's approach in real time, and enjoy the ease of cashless payments.

Ride-sharing services offer the added advantage of transparency, with fare estimates provided upfront, eliminating the uncertainty that sometimes accompanies traditional taxi rides. This modern approach to transportation aligns with the contemporary pulse of the city, allowing you to seamlessly navigate Malaga's urban landscape with the aid of technology.

Exploring Freedom: The Choice is Yours

Whether you opt for a taxi or a ride-sharing service, both options grant you the freedom to explore Malaga without the hassle of parking or the stress of navigating unfamiliar streets. They provide a tailored travel experience, allowing you to chart your course through the city's offerings at your own pace and according to your preferences.

As you travel in the company of Malaga's taxis or ride-sharing services, you're not just moving from place to place; you're immersing yourself in the flow of urban life, engaging with the city's rhythm, and savoring every moment of discovery. The symphony of the streets, the scents of local cuisine, and the vibrant energy of the people become part of your journey, shaping your experience in ways that resonate long after you've reached your final destination.

1.3 Recommended Local Apps For Booking Transport

When it comes to booking transport in Malaga and exploring the Costa del Sol, there are several local apps that can enhance your travel experience and make navigating the region more convenient. Here are some recommended apps that you might find useful:

TaxiMalaga: This app allows you to easily book taxis in Malaga. It provides real-time information about nearby available taxis, estimated fares, and the ability to track your taxi's location as it approaches your pickup point. TaxiMalaga streamlines the process of hailing a taxi and makes getting around the city hassle-free.

MyTaxi: Similar to TaxiMalaga, MyTaxi is another app that connects you with local taxi services. It offers features like ride tracking, estimated fares, and secure payment options. The app often provides additional information about drivers, helping you choose the most suitable ride for your needs.

Bicimálaga: For those interested in cycling around the city, Bicimálaga offers information about the city's bike-sharing system. This app provides details about bike station locations, bike availability, and even allows you to reserve a bike in advance. It's a great tool for exploring Malaga on two wheels.

EMT Malaga: If you're planning to use the city's buses, the EMT Malaga app provides real-time bus tracking, routes, schedules, and service alerts. This app helps you plan your bus journeys efficiently, ensuring you reach your destinations without unnecessary wait times.

RENFE Cercanías: If you're planning to use the local train services, the RENFE Cercanías app provides information about the local commuter trains connecting various destinations within the Costa del Sol region. It offers schedules, route maps, and real-time updates to help you navigate the train network.

Uber: While not a local app, Uber operates in Malaga and other major cities in Spain. If you're already familiar with the Uber platform, using the app can provide a convenient and familiar way to book rides around the city and beyond.

Cabify: Similar to Uber, Cabify is another ride-sharing app available in Malaga. It offers comfortable rides with professional drivers and provides a reliable way to move around the city and explore nearby areas.

Before your trip, it's a good idea to download these apps and familiarize yourself with their features. Having these tools at your disposal can greatly enhance your travel experience, making it easier to book transport, explore the region, and fully immerse yourself in the charms of Malaga and the Costa del Sol.

Whether you prefer the convenience of public transportation or the freedom of a rental car, the transportation options in Malaga and the Costa del Sol cater to various travel styles, making it easy to navigate the region and explore its enchanting charms.

CHAPTER TWO

MALAGA: PICASSO'S HOMETOWN AND BEYOND

2.1 Unveiling the Rich Heritage of Malaga

Malaga, a coastal gem nestled in the heart of Andalusia, Spain, boasts a heritage that spans millennia, a tapestry intricately woven with threads of history, art, and culture. As you step into this vibrant city, you embark on a voyage through time, immersing yourself in a legacy that dates back to ancient civilizations. From the Phoenicians and Romans to the Moors and Christians, each era has contributed to the captivating mosaic that defines Malaga's landscape and character.

Ancient Echoes: Tracing the Footsteps of Civilizations

Malaga's origins are intertwined with those of the Phoenicians, a seafaring people who established a trading post here around 770 BC. Their presence marked the first chapter in the city's story, laying the foundation for its future as a thriving cultural hub. The remnants of their settlement can still be glimpsed in archaeological sites, echoing tales of maritime commerce and exchange.

Following the Phoenicians, the Romans arrived in the 3rd century BC, leaving their indelible mark on the region. Their influence is evident in the ruins of the Roman Theater, an ancient amphitheater that once resonated with the cheers of spectators. This historic site stands as a silent witness to the spectacles of the past, inviting visitors to imagine the vibrant performances that once graced its stage.

The Moors' Enduring Legacy: Architecture and Artistry

The Moors, who arrived in the 8th century AD, brought with them an era of innovation and cultural fusion that would shape Malaga's identity for centuries to come. Their architectural prowess is showcased in the breathtaking Alcazaba Fortress, an intricate network of walls and gardens that rises above the city. This imposing stronghold not only served as a defensive bastion but also as a testament to the Moors' mastery of design and engineering.

Adjacent to the Alcazaba stands Gibralfaro Castle, a symbol of the Moors' architectural brilliance. The castle's strategic hilltop location offers sweeping views of the city and the Mediterranean, serving as a reminder of the Moors' strategic acumen and their harmonious integration of the natural landscape into their constructions.

A Renaissance of Culture: From Gothic to Modern Marvels

As the centuries unfolded, Malaga witnessed the transition from Moorish rule to Christian influence. This shift brought about a period of architectural renaissance, where Gothic cathedrals and Renaissance facades began to adorn the city's skyline. The Malaga Cathedral, an embodiment of this architectural evolution, stands as a testament to the city's ability to adapt and transform.

The fusion of cultures is most evident in the Old Town's architecture. Narrow alleys wind their way past Gothic churches, Moorish arches, and neoclassical facades. Each corner turned reveals a new layer of history, a narrative etched into the very fabric of the city. This rich tapestry of architectural styles stands as a tribute to Malaga's ability to embrace diverse influences while maintaining its distinct character.

Conclusion: A Heritage Beyond Time

Malaga's heritage is not confined to the pages of history books; it lives and breathes within the city's streets, monuments, and people. The legacy of Phoenicians, Romans, Moors, and Christians converges to create an intricate mosaic that transcends time. As you explore the streets lined with architectural marvels, you're not merely a spectator; you become a part of this ongoing narrative, connecting with the past while charting a course for the future. In Malaga, the echoes of ancient civilizations harmonize with the rhythms of modern life, creating a symphony that resonates in the hearts of all who visit this enchanting city.

2.2 Exploring the Picasso Museum and Tracing the Artist's Roots

No exploration of Malaga's rich heritage can be considered complete without embarking on a journey through the life and artistic legacy of its most celebrated native, Pablo Picasso. As a city that has nurtured and inspired one of the greatest artists of all time, Malaga opens its heart to those who seek to understand the man behind the masterpieces. The Picasso Museum, nestled in the heart of the city, stands as a testament to his genius, offering a captivating voyage through the evolution of his art and the essence of his creative spirit.

A Sanctuary of Creativity: The Picasso Museum

Located in the heart of Malaga's historic district, the Picasso Museum is a sanctuary where visitors can immerse themselves in the world of the artist. The museum itself is a work of art, housed within the beautifully restored Palacio de Buenavista, a 16th-century Andalusian palace. As you step through its doors, you enter a realm where time seems to blur, and you're transported to the various phases of Picasso's prolific career.

The museum's collection is a treasure trove that spans Picasso's lifetime, offering a remarkable insight into his creative journey. From the earliest sketches that reveal the artist's formative years to the iconic masterpieces that have left an indelible mark on art history, every brushstroke tells a story. The breadth and depth of the collection allow visitors to witness the evolution of Picasso's artistic language, from his Blue and Rose Periods to the radical innovations of Cubism and beyond.

Tracing Picasso's Roots: A Glimpse into his Origins

Tracing the footsteps of Picasso through the museum is a journey that transcends artistic appreciation—it's a glimpse into the very soul of the artist. Here, in the city of his birth, you can connect with the influences that shaped his unique perspective on the world. You'll gain insights into the cultural milieu in which he was raised, the familial ties that shaped his early years, and the encounters that ignited his creative spark.

Malaga's influence on Picasso is profound. The Mediterranean light that bathes the city's streets and shores finds its way onto his canvases, infusing them with a luminosity that is both evocative and enchanting. The vibrant colors and dynamic compositions of his works are a reflection of the city's energy and the artistic atmosphere that permeated his surroundings.

The Creative Spirit of Malaga: An Ongoing Legacy

Standing before Picasso's artworks in the museum, you become more than an observer; you become a participant in the dialogue between the artist and his audience. The vivid strokes, the bold experiments, and the emotive subjects all come to life, bridging the gap between the past and the present. Picasso's creative spirit continues to reverberate through the city's streets, galleries, and cultural events, reminding all who visit that Malaga is not merely a place of historical significance, but a thriving hub of artistic inspiration.

Beyond the walls of the museum, you can explore the very landscapes that once ignited Picasso's imagination. Wander through the bustling streets where he once walked, discovering the sights and scenes that undoubtedly found their way onto his canvases. As you take in the city's vibrant energy, you're enveloped by a palpable sense of creativity—a testament to the enduring impact of Picasso's legacy on Malaga's cultural fabric.

Conclusion: Picasso's Enduring Legacy

In Malaga, Pablo Picasso's presence is more than a historical footnote; it's a living, breathing force that shapes the city's identity and enriches the lives of those who visit. The Picasso Museum stands not just as a repository of art but as a portal into the mind of a genius who redefined artistic expression. As you explore the museum's halls and encounter the diverse works that chart Picasso's evolution, you're invited to embark on a journey of introspection and inspiration. The essence of Malaga's creative spirit, embodied in Picasso's art, continues to captivate the world, leaving an indelible mark on all who seek to understand the complexities of human expression.

2.3 Roaming the Alcazaba Fortress and Gibralfaro Castle

Sentinels of History: Alcazaba Fortress and Gibralfaro Castle in Malaga

Perched high atop the enchanting city of Malaga, the Alcazaba Fortress and Gibralfaro Castle stand as steadfast guardians of its illustrious past. These formidable structures, each with its own tale to tell, offer visitors a glimpse into the history, culture, and architectural prowess that have shaped Malaga's identity over the centuries. As you ascend to these historic heights, you embark on a journey through time, immersing yourself in the remnants of a bygone era while being rewarded with awe-inspiring views that span across the city and the boundless Mediterranean Sea.

The Alcazaba Fortress: A Majestic Moorish Legacy

As you approach the Alcazaba Fortress, it becomes evident that this majestic edifice holds the secrets of Malaga's Moorish heritage within its walls. Constructed during the 11th century, the Alcazaba stands as a testament to the architectural ingenuity of its creators. Its very presence conjures images of a time when fortified citadels were as much a statement of power as they were a place of refuge.

Upon entering the Alcazaba, you are transported to a different era, surrounded by ornate courtyards, intricate archways, and lush gardens that evoke the opulence of Al-Andalus. The interplay of light and shadow casts a spell, inviting you to explore its labyrinthine corridors and imagine the lives that once unfolded within these walls. Every stone carries the whispers of the past, connecting you to the generations that have sought solace and inspiration within this hallowed fortress.

The Alcazaba's vantage point offers panoramic views that stretch from the bustling streets below to the azure expanse of the Mediterranean beyond. As you gaze out from its ramparts, you're rewarded with a perspective that transcends time, reminding you of the fortress's strategic significance as a protector of the city and its inhabitants.

Gibralfaro Castle: A Bastion of History and Beauty

Connected to the Alcazaba by a scenic pathway, Gibralfaro Castle presents another layer of Malaga's history waiting to be uncovered. The castle's name itself—derived from the Arabic "Jabal-Faruk," meaning "Rock of the Lighthouse"—harks back to its origins atop the ruins of a Phoenician lighthouse. The castle, fortified during the Nasrid dynasty, stands as a testament to the strategic importance of the high ground it occupies.

Exploring the towers and walls of Gibralfaro Castle is a journey through time, as you traverse the steps that generations before you once walked. As you ascend its heights, the reward is twofold: historical insights and breathtaking vistas. From its watchtowers, the panorama unfolds before you—an uninterrupted view that stretches across the city, the harbor, and the endless stretch of the Mediterranean Sea. The convergence of land and sea becomes a painter's palette, painted with the hues of the changing skies and shimmering waters.

A Journey Through Time and Vision

Visiting the Alcazaba Fortress and Gibralfaro Castle is not merely an exploration of stone and architecture; it's a journey through time and vision. These structures are more than just relics of the past; they're living testaments to the resilience, creativity, and determination of those who came before us. They remind us that history is not a distant echo but a living, breathing force that shapes the present and influences the future.

As you descend from these historic heights, you carry with you the echoes of battles fought and victories won, the whispers of stories that have stood the test of time. The panoramic views etched in your memory serve as a reminder of the beauty and grandeur that continue to captivate all who gaze upon Malaga's horizon. The Alcazaba Fortress and Gibralfaro Castle are not just monuments; they're gateways to a deeper understanding of the city's soul, an invitation to connect with the essence of Malaga's rich and enduring heritage.

2.4 Strolling Through the Lively Streets of Malaga's Old Town

Nestled within the heart of Malaga, the Old Town is a haven of captivating stories, where the whispers of centuries past meld seamlessly with the vibrant rhythms of the present. Every step taken through its labyrinthine streets is a step back in time, a chance to explore the tapestry of Malaga's heritage woven with threads of old-world charm and modern vivacity. The Old Town, with its cobblestone pathways, picturesque squares, and a symphony of aromas, invites you to embark on a journey that transcends time.

A Tapestry of Architecture and Atmosphere

The Old Town is more than a geographical area; it's a living testament to the layers of history that have shaped Malaga's identity. With every corner turned, you're transported to a different era, from the winding alleys reminiscent of Moorish influence to the grand squares that reflect the city's Renaissance heritage.

Narrow lanes reveal hidden plazas where locals gather, sharing stories and laughter against a backdrop of centuries-old architecture. These squares, with their charming fountains and inviting benches, provide a serene respite from the bustling energy of the city. The contrast between the modern world and the echoes of antiquity is striking, creating an atmosphere that is at once familiar and utterly enchanting.

Cafes, Boutiques, and Artisan Delights

The Old Town is a treasure trove of sensory delights, where the senses are awakened at every turn. Quaint cafes spill out onto the cobblestones, offering a front-row seat to the theater of daily life. Here, you can indulge in the simple pleasure of people-watching while sipping on a cup of aromatic coffee or a refreshing glass of local wine. The gentle clink of glasses mingles with the soft hum of conversation, creating a symphony that serenades your senses.

Boutiques and artisan shops dot the streets, showcasing the city's rich tradition of craftsmanship. Each shop window is a gallery of handmade treasures—jewelry, textiles, ceramics—that bear the mark of meticulous attention to detail. These items tell stories of local artisans who have honed their craft over generations, ensuring that Malaga's artistic heritage continues to thrive.

A Culinary Odyssey: Tapas and Gastronomic Adventures

No exploration of Malaga's Old Town is complete without savoring its culinary offerings. The aroma of tapas permeates the air, guiding your senses toward the myriad of flavors waiting to be savored. Tapas, the heart and soul of Spanish cuisine, are an invitation to indulge in bite-sized wonders that reflect the region's culinary diversity.

As you meander through the Old Town's alleys, you'll encounter taverns and restaurants that beckon with an array of tapas, from traditional to innovative. Each bite is a journey through Andalusia's culinary landscape, where fresh ingredients and time-honored recipes come together in a symphony of taste.

An Unforgettable Journey Through Heritage

Wandering through Malaga's Old Town isn't merely a sightseeing endeavor; it's an immersive experience that invites you to step into the rhythm of the city's soul. The history and vibrancy of this area converge to create an atmosphere that is both captivating and authentic. With every footstep, you become part of the narrative, part of the living heritage that has been passed down through generations.

The Old Town isn't confined to the past; it's a vibrant hub where history and modernity dance together. It's a celebration of Malaga's ability to honor its roots while embracing the present, an embodiment of the city's enduring spirit. As you bid farewell to its enchanting streets, you take with you not just memories of stunning architecture and delectable flavors, but a deep appreciation for the rich tapestry of life that defines Malaga's Old Town—a place where history and vibrancy intertwine, leaving an indelible mark on all who tread its paths.

CHAPTER THREE
SUN-KISSED BEACHES AND COASTAL DELIGHTS

3.1 Discovering the Best Beaches along the Costa del Sol

The Costa del Sol is renowned for its stunning coastline, boasting an array of picturesque beaches that cater to various preferences. Whether you're seeking vibrant beach parties or tranquil sunsets, this region has it all.

3.1.1 Playa de la Malagueta:

Nestled within arm's reach of Malaga's bustling city center, the captivating Playa de la Malagueta emerges as a cherished jewel along the Costa del Sol. This sun-kissed haven, a beguiling urban beach, extends a warm invitation to both locals and visitors seeking a respite from the city's lively rhythm. With its soft, golden sands and crystalline waters, Playa de la Malagueta casts a spell that effortlessly captivates families, couples, and solo travelers alike.

A Coastal Retreat Amidst the Urban Pulse

Playa de la Malagueta stands as an enchanting testament to the harmonious coexistence of the city's vivacity and the tranquil allure of the Mediterranean coast. Just a leisurely stroll from the heart of Malaga's city center, this beach represents a seamless fusion of convenience and natural beauty. The convenience factor cannot be understated, making it an accessible getaway for those craving the sun and the sea without embarking on extensive journeys.

A Tapestry of Sands and Waters

Upon stepping onto Playa de la Malagueta, visitors are greeted by a sprawling tapestry of soft sands that seem to stretch infinitely towards the horizon. The sands are a canvas for sunbathers, families building sandcastles, and friends engaged in jovial beach games. As the waves gently kiss the shore, the azure waters shimmer under the Mediterranean sun, creating an idyllic setting for swimmers and water enthusiasts to cool off and revel in nature's embrace.

A Haven for Families and Couples

The allure of Playa de la Malagueta is heightened by its suitability for a diverse array of visitors. Families with children find solace in its shores, as the gradual slope of the beach into the sea creates a safe haven for youngsters to splash and play. Couples, in search of romantic interludes, are beckoned by the enchanting ambiance, perfect for leisurely walks along the shoreline and intimate moments basking in the beauty of the surroundings.

Proximity to Amenities and Culinary Delights

One of the undeniable charms of Playa de la Malagueta is its proximity to the city's amenities. The beachgoer's comfort is enhanced by the availability of nearby conveniences, ensuring that the experience is as relaxing as possible. Cafes, bars, and restaurants line the promenade, offering respite in the form of refreshing drinks, delectable snacks, and sumptuous meals. The opportunity to savor the local culinary delights while gazing at the ocean horizon is an experience that paints lasting memories.

The Subtle Magic of Sunset

As the sun begins its descent into the tranquil waters, Playa de la Malagueta undergoes a transformation that can only be described as magical. The soft hues of orange, pink, and gold cast a warm glow over the beach, turning the sands into a sea of captivating colors. Couples walking hand in hand, families engaged in laughter, and solo wanderers lost in contemplation all find themselves drawn to the beach's edge to witness this breathtaking spectacle. The beauty of a Malaga sunset experienced from Playa de la Malagueta is a memory etched in the heart forever.

In the heart of bustling Malaga, Playa de la Malagueta beckons with its promise of sun-soaked serenity. Its soft sands, clear waters, and convenient location create an irresistible magnetism that lures visitors seeking relaxation, family fun, romantic moments, and culinary delights. Whether it's a tranquil morning stroll, a day of joyful beach activities, or a mesmerizing sunset, Playa de la Malagueta stands as a testament to the harmonious blend of urban dynamism and coastal enchantment.

3.1.2 Playa de la Misericordia:
Nestled as another precious gem within the vibrant city of Malaga, Playa de la Misericordia stretches majestically over two kilometers, offering a serene retreat for both locals and visitors. This tranquil expanse of coastline is revered for its impeccable sandy shores and the gentle embrace of its calm waves. However, its allure extends beyond the mere beauty

of nature – it presents an inviting escape, a haven of tranquility that beckons those seeking solace from the everyday hustle and bustle.

A Canvas of Pristine Sands and Calm Waters

Playa de la Misericordia, with its seemingly endless stretch of fine golden sands, presents a canvas that entices beachgoers to shed their worries and immerse themselves in the simple pleasures of life. The sands, soft and inviting, cradle the footsteps of those seeking to bask in the sun's warm embrace. The waters, an exquisite shade of blue, stretch into the horizon, inviting swimmers and waders to experience a gentle communion with the Mediterranean's soothing waters. It's a place where the boundaries between sky, sea, and land blur, creating a timeless scene of serenity.

The Symphony of Leisurely Strolls

While the waves whisper their melodies along the shoreline, Playa de la Misericordia's most enchanting feature might well be its promenade. This charming walkway extends like a ribbon alongside the beach, offering a perfect avenue for leisurely strolls and contemplative moments. As the sun dips below the horizon, casting hues of gold and orange across the water, couples saunter hand in hand, families create lasting memories, and individuals find respite in the rhythmic lapping of waves against the shore. It's a place where time seems to slow down, allowing one to savor the present and disconnect from the hurried world beyond.

A Culinary Voyage Along the Promenade

The allure of Playa de la Misericordia doesn't end with its natural beauty; it seamlessly blends with the vibrancy of local culture and gastronomy. The promenade acts as a boulevard of flavors, where the aroma of local delicacies mingles with the salty sea breeze. From traditional tapas to delectable seafood dishes, the nearby local eateries offer a gastronomic voyage that mirrors the journey of the waves – both comforting and invigorating. Dining alfresco along the promenade is an experience that engages all the senses, combining taste, sight, and sound in a symphony of culinary delight.

An Oasis of Tranquility

Playa de la Misericordia stands as an oasis of tranquility within the bustling heart of Malaga. Amid the city's dynamic energy and vibrant culture, this beach offers a gentle reprieve – a place where the relentless rhythms of urban life fade into the background. Whether one seeks the warmth of the sun's rays, the soothing embrace of the sea, or the solace of a leisurely stroll, Playa de la Misericordia invites all to embark on a journey of inner renewal.

A Sanctuary for the Soul

With its pristine sands, calm waters, and the symphony of the promenade, Playa de la Misericordia is more than just a beach; it's a sanctuary for the soul. It's a reminder that even in the midst of a bustling city, pockets of serenity exist, waiting to be discovered by those who yearn for a moment of respite. As the sun sets and the stars begin to twinkle, Playa de la Misericordia continues to weave its gentle magic, offering an escape from the ordinary and an invitation to embrace the extraordinary simplicity of nature's beauty.

3.2 Engaging in Water Sports and Activities for Thrill-Seekers

For those seeking an adrenaline rush and an active beach experience, the Costa del Sol doesn't disappoint. From water sports to thrilling activities, there's something for every adventure enthusiast.

3.2.1 Waterskiing and Wakeboarding:

Amidst the gentle embrace of the Mediterranean's tranquil waters, a world of exhilarating aquatic experiences beckons the adventurous spirit. Waterskiing and wakeboarding, two adrenaline-pumping pursuits, find their natural playground on these serene waves, offering enthusiasts a taste of excitement and a chance to conquer the seascape's challenges. While the Costa del Sol brims with alluring options for aquatic thrills, Marbella and Fuengirola stand as the dynamic epicenters of these invigorating activities, inviting thrill-seekers to ride the waves and create memories that will ripple through time.

Embracing the Challenge: Waterskiing and Wakeboarding

Waterskiing and wakeboarding are more than mere water sports – they are feats of harmony between human skill and natural elements. As the sun's rays dance upon the glistening sea, enthusiasts step onto their boards, ready to embrace the challenge. Waterskiing involves skimming the water's surface, pulled along by a motorboat's propulsive force, while wakeboarding requires balancing atop a board as a cable system or boat propels them forward. The feel of the water rushing beneath, the wind in one's face, and the promise of conquering the waves all contribute to the rush of adrenaline that accompanies these experiences.

Marbella: Where Adventure Meets Luxury

In Marbella, where luxury meets adventure, waterskiing and wakeboarding find their canvas in the calm, cerulean waters that gently kiss the coastline. Marbella's reputation as a playground for the elite extends beyond the shores, as the waters offer the perfect setting for thrilling aquatic endeavors. For those seeking to combine the exhilaration of watersports with the luxury the city is known for, Marbella presents a formidable option. The seamless transition from the heart of the city to the beckoning waves highlights the allure of this coastal haven.

Fuengirola: A Haven for Aquatic Enthusiasts

Fuengirola, with its charismatic blend of history and modernity, also stands as a haven for aquatic enthusiasts seeking the thrill of waterskiing and wakeboarding. The Mediterranean's gentle waves provide the ideal playground for those eager to ride the water's surface and experience the unique rush that only these sports can deliver. Fuengirola's dedication to recreational pursuits, combined with its vibrant atmosphere, creates a backdrop that encourages both novices and seasoned riders to take on the challenge and revel in the waters' embrace.

Beyond the Sport: A Symphony of Experiences

Waterskiing and wakeboarding transcend the boundaries of mere sport; they offer a symphony of experiences that engage both body and spirit. The rhythmic dance between human will and the water's currents creates a harmony that resonates deep within, evoking a profound connection to the natural world. As the waves rise and fall, riders navigate with finesse and determination, finding an exhilaration that is not solely about speed, but about mastery and immersion in the elements.

Unveiling Boundless Horizons

Marbella and Fuengirola, nestled along the Costa del Sol, stand as gateways to boundless horizons of aquatic adventure. Waterskiing and wakeboarding, amidst the calm Mediterranean waters, invite enthusiasts to push their limits, challenge their fears, and embrace the rush of adrenaline. Beyond the invigorating thrills, these experiences offer a unique perspective on the sea, a dance of balance and motion that connects riders with the timeless rhythm of the ocean. So, whether one is carving through the waves for the first time or mastering intricate maneuvers, the Costa del Sol's waters promise an unforgettable journey into the heart of aquatic exhilaration.

3.2.2 Kite Surfing and Wind Surfing:

Along the sun-kissed shores of the Costa del Sol, a thrilling world of wind and waves unfolds, inviting adventurers to harness the power of the elements and embark on exhilarating journeys atop the water. Kite surfing and wind surfing, two electrifying water sports, find their ultimate haven on this Mediterranean coastline, where the consistent winds and favorable conditions create a paradise for those seeking to soar on the seas. Amidst this aquatic tapestry of possibilities, Tarifa stands tall as a beacon of wind and wave, acclaimed as not just a destination, but a shrine to kite surfing excellence, making the Costa del Sol a revered hub for these high-energy aquatic pursuits.

A Symphony of Elements: Kite Surfing and Wind Surfing Defined

Kite surfing and wind surfing are more than just sports; they are harmonious symphonies played by the wind, the waves, and the riders themselves. These activities demand a union of skill and intuition as enthusiasts glide across the water's surface, propelled by the wind's invisible hand. Kite surfing enthusiasts navigate the waves while controlling a kite, using its power to propel themselves into gravity-defying jumps and maneuvers. Wind surfers, on the other hand, ride a board attached to a sail, manipulating the wind's force to glide with grace and speed across the water.

Costa del Sol: A Playground for Wind Lovers

The Costa del Sol, with its gentle winds and inviting waters, presents the perfect backdrop for kite surfing and wind surfing enthusiasts to chase their aquatic dreams. Wind, consistent and reliable, weaves through the air, creating an arena where riders can master the art of sailing on water with finesse and flair. This region's unique blend of wind conditions and mild climate has earned it a reputation as a haven for wind lovers, with the Costa del Sol's waves and winds serving as a thrilling canvas for the pursuit of these dynamic sports.

Tarifa: The Epicenter of Kite Surfing Excellence

Nestled at the southernmost tip of Spain, the coastal town of Tarifa emerges as a legendary destination for kite surfing, capturing the hearts of enthusiasts from around the globe. Its fame as one of Europe's premier kite surfing spots is well-deserved, owed to its perfect marriage of wind patterns, warm waters, and vibrant culture. Tarifa's beaches, kissed by both the Mediterranean and the Atlantic, offer riders a diverse range of conditions, from gentle breezes to invigorating gusts, ensuring that beginners and experts alike can find their rhythm and challenge their limits.

Beyond the Thrill: A Spiritual Dance

Kite surfing and wind surfing are more than extreme sports; they're spiritual dances that connect riders with the rhythm of nature. The wind, the water, and the rider become one in a harmonious display of grace and power. The exhilaration of gliding across the water, propelled by unseen forces, brings a unique sense of freedom and accomplishment that lingers long after the waves have settled. Whether you're a novice seeking your first taste of adventure or an experienced rider looking to push your boundaries, the Costa del Sol's windswept waters provide a sanctuary to experience this remarkable fusion of elements.

A Bond with Nature: Embracing the Elements

The Costa del Sol, with its gentle winds and welcoming waters, serves as an open invitation for kite surfers and wind surfers to establish a bond with nature that's both exhilarating and humbling. These aquatic pursuits not only offer an escape from the ordinary but also a chance to embrace the extraordinary through a fusion of athleticism, skill, and an intimate connection with the elements. As riders glide across the waves, dancing with the wind, they experience a unique kind of freedom that reminds them of the profound beauty and power of the natural world.

3.3 Relaxing in Charming Coastal Villages: Nerja, Marbella, and Beyond

The Costa del Sol is not only about bustling cities but also charming coastal villages that exude a laid-back vibe and old-world charm. Here are a few you won't want to miss.

3.3.1 Nerja:

Nestled harmoniously along the sun-kissed coast, the charming town of Nerja stands as a coastal gem that beckons travelers with its irresistible blend of natural wonders and cultural riches. This idyllic destination captures the essence of Andalusian beauty, boasting a palette that includes stunning beaches, a world-renowned promenade called the Balcony of Europe, and a subterranean marvel known as the Nerja Caves. Within the embrace of Nerja's embrace, visitors are transported into a world where time seems to stand still, where every moment is a canvas of exploration and awe.

Beaches of Unspoiled Splendor

Nerja's beaches are a testament to the mesmerizing beauty of the Mediterranean. These stretches of golden sands are more than just places to soak up the sun; they are invitations to immerse oneself in the soothing embrace of the sea. Playa Burriana, with its azure waters and array of water sports, caters to the adventurer in search of action. For those craving tranquility, Playa Calahonda offers a secluded cove with pristine sands, perfect for basking in the sun's glow while the gentle lapping of waves creates a lullaby of serenity.

The Balcony of Europe: A Panoramic Marvel

As if plucked from a dream, the Balcony of Europe emerges as an enchanting promenade that stretches out over the cerulean expanse, offering panoramic vistas that defy description. Perched atop a natural headland, this iconic spot provides an unobstructed view of the Mediterranean's vastness, a canvas painted with shades of blue that seem to merge with the sky on the distant horizon. From sunrise to sunset, the Balcony of Europe is a place of contemplation and wonder, inviting travelers to lose themselves in the poetic beauty of the sea meeting the sky.

The Subterranean Realm of the Nerja Caves

Beneath Nerja's picturesque surface lies a realm of wonder that seems to belong to another world entirely. The Nerja Caves, a subterranean complex of chambers adorned with awe-inspiring stalactites and stalagmites, hold a captivating allure. These natural formations, meticulously crafted by time and water, create a labyrinth of wonder that captivates the imagination. The haunting beauty of these formations, illuminated in a soft, ethereal glow, conjures a sense of reverence, reminding visitors of the profound mysteries that lie beneath the surface of our planet.

A Journey Beyond Time

In Nerja, every step is a journey beyond time, a chance to experience a harmonious blend of natural splendor and historical significance. The town's welcoming spirit, coupled with its breathtaking landscapes, creates a tapestry of experiences that linger in the heart. From the mesmerizing beaches that soothe the soul to the Balcony of Europe's embrace of boundless horizons, and the Nerja Caves' descent into the Earth's secrets, Nerja presents a symphony of elements that invite travelers to explore, discover, and marvel at the wonders of the world around them.

A Tapestry of Beauty and Discovery

Nerja's allure is more than just skin deep; it's a tapestry woven from the threads of beauty and discovery. It's a destination that unveils the delicate balance between natural landscapes and human appreciation, where the splendor of the Mediterranean is mirrored in the town's timeless charm. In Nerja, visitors embark on a journey that transcends the ordinary, a journey that invites them to embrace the world's beauty in all its forms and revel in the awe-inspiring wonders that lie at every turn.

3.3.2 Marbella:

Amidst the glitz and glamour that have come to define Marbella's luxurious reputation, a hidden gem awaits, tucked away within the embrace of history and charm. Marbella's Old Town, a veritable labyrinth of narrow streets and historic edifices, stands as a testament to the town's enduring allure and rich heritage. Here, amidst the polished façade of modern luxury, a slice of the past beckons, inviting travelers to wander through its time-worn alleys, admire its architectural treasures, and immerse themselves in a picturesque haven of elegance.

A Glimpse into the Past: Meandering Through History

The Old Town of Marbella is a living canvas that transports visitors to a bygone era, where the pace of life was slower, and every cobblestone seemed to hold stories of its own. As one navigates the labyrinthine pathways, a sense of timelessness permeates the air. The architecture is a blend of styles, reflecting the town's Moorish and Andalusian roots. Whitewashed buildings adorned with wrought-iron balconies create a harmonious aesthetic, transporting visitors into a world where the past effortlessly intertwines with the present.

A Jewel of Restful Tranquility

In the heart of Marbella's Old Town, the bustling energy of the modern world seems to fade into a distant echo. The narrow streets, bathed in the golden glow of sunlight, exude a sense of intimacy and tranquility that offers respite from the outside world. Locals leisurely stroll along, exchanging greetings with familiar faces, and travelers find themselves captivated by the sense of community that thrives within these streets. Amidst the ancient walls, Marbella's Old Town becomes a haven of serenity, inviting visitors to pause, breathe, and truly experience the art of being present.

A Blend of Sophistication and Relaxed Charm

While Marbella's luxurious reputation precedes it, the Old Town presents a different facet of the town's character – one that is steeped in relaxed charm and understated elegance. Beyond the glitz, the town's historic heart provides a haven where the soul can find solace in simplicity. Marbella's beaches, too, echo this blend of sophistication and relaxation. The sun-kissed shores are adorned with chaise lounges and umbrellas that invite sun-seekers to unwind and savor the Mediterranean bliss. The rhythm of the waves, the salty breeze, and the sensation of warm sands underfoot combine to create a sensory symphony that envelops visitors in a soothing embrace.

A Timeless Invitation

Marbella's Old Town is more than just a collection of buildings; it's a timeless invitation to immerse oneself in the fabric of history. It's a reminder that beneath the veneer of luxury lies a soul that is deeply rooted in its past, and that the heart of a town is often found in the quaintest corners. As the modern world rushes by, the Old Town remains steadfast, inviting travelers to step into its embrace, slow down, and savor the simple pleasures of discovery. It's a place where the echoes of history reverberate in the wind, where the beauty of yesterday intertwines with the vitality of today, and where each step is an exploration of the soul of Marbella.

3.3.3 Estepona:

Nestled along the coastline of the Costa del Sol, the quaint village of Estepona emerges as a true gem, exuding the authentic essence of Andalusia's captivating charm. With a seafront promenade that seems to have sprung from a canvas of dreams, adorned with a vibrant array of colorful flowerpots, Estepona creates a scene that is both enchanting and inviting. Here, amidst the gentle lapping of the Mediterranean waves, visitors have the opportunity to step into the heart of the authentic Andalusian way of life, where simplicity reigns, and every moment unfolds with a touch of timeless magic.

A Symphony of Colors: The Seafront Promenade

The seafront promenade of Estepona is a testament to the town's commitment to beauty and community. As if competing with the azure of the Mediterranean, colorful flowerpots line the pathways, creating an enchanting tapestry that blends nature's vibrant palette with the simple elegance of white-washed walls. Bougainvillea, geraniums, and hibiscus spill over the edges of terracotta pots, adding bursts of red, pink, and orange to the scene. Each step along the promenade is an immersion in a symphony of colors, a dance of hues that awaken the senses and evoke a feeling of joy.

A Glimpse into Authentic Andalusian Life

Beyond its picturesque appearance, Estepona's seafront promenade offers a rare glimpse into the heart of authentic Andalusian life. As visitors wander along the cobblestone pathways, they find themselves immersed in a world where time moves at its own unhurried pace, and the joys of community and connection are celebrated. Locals engage in lively conversations on benches overlooking the sea, families gather for picnics, and children play along the waterfront, creating an atmosphere of kinship that is both heartwarming and inspiring.

A Sanctuary of Simplicity and Serenity

Estepona's seafront promenade is a sanctuary for those seeking to escape the chaos of modern life and find solace in simplicity. The gentle sound of waves brushing against the shore becomes a backdrop for contemplation and relaxation. Visitors are invited to slow down, to savor the moment, and to appreciate the beauty of a world where nature and humanity coexist in harmonious balance. The promenade becomes a canvas of tranquility, offering a space to reflect, to rejuvenate, and to immerse oneself in the rhythms of the sea and the spirit of the village.

An Invitation to Wander

Estepona's seafront promenade isn't just a place to stroll; it's an invitation to wander with purpose, to connect with the essence of Andalusia, and to embrace the gentle pleasures of life. The colorful flowerpots, the scent of the sea, and the laughter of locals combine to create an atmosphere that is rich with authenticity and charm. As the sun dips below the horizon, casting warm hues across the water, the promenade transforms into a space where memories are woven, where hearts are lightened, and where the true beauty of Estepona's spirit is revealed.

A Window to the Soul of Estepona

The seafront promenade of Estepona isn't just a pathway; it's a window to the soul of the village. It's a place where simplicity is revered, where nature is celebrated, and where the bonds of community are cherished. As visitors take in the breathtaking colors, the soothing sounds, and the palpable sense of belonging, they are drawn into a world that transcends time and resonates with the core of human experience. Estepona's seafront promenade invites all to step into its embrace, to bask in its beauty, and to experience the heart of Andalusia in every step taken along its enchanting pathways.

3.3.4 Fuengirola:

Nestled along the sun-drenched Costa del Sol, Fuengirola emerges as a vibrant tapestry of experiences that cater to both the young and the young at heart. This charming coastal town is more than just a destination; it's an open invitation to families seeking the perfect blend of relaxation and entertainment. With bustling markets, inviting beaches, and a collection of charming squares, Fuengirola transforms into a haven where cherished memories are woven, where laughter echoes through the streets, and where the spirit of togetherness is celebrated at every turn.

A Vibrant Melting Pot: The Bustling Markets

Fuengirola's markets are like vibrant bazaars, offering a glimpse into the heart of local life and culture. The Mercado de Fuengirola, with its stalls brimming with fresh produce, artisanal goods, and vibrant flowers, becomes a symphony of colors and scents that awaken the senses. Families can wander through the aisles, engaging with local vendors, sampling delicacies, and discovering treasures that embody the spirit of the region. It's a journey that bridges generations, where children learn about the essence of community and the importance of supporting local businesses.

Charming Squares: Where Stories Unfold

Fuengirola's charming squares are more than just architectural landmarks; they're vibrant hubs of life and laughter. Plaza de la Constitución, the heart of the town, stands as a gathering place where families can bask in the warmth of the sun, savoring local treats from nearby cafes while watching children play. The square becomes a canvas for impromptu performances, joyful celebrations, and moments of connection that remind everyone of the simple pleasures of being together. In Fuengirola's squares, history blends seamlessly with modern life, creating an atmosphere that invites families to create their own stories against a backdrop of centuries-old charm.

Seaside Bliss: The Inviting Beaches

Fuengirola's coastline offers more than just pristine shores; it presents a playground of relaxation and fun for families. The inviting beaches become a canvas for endless adventures, where children build sandcastles, splash in the gentle waves, and embark on seashell hunts. Parents can unwind under the shade of beach umbrellas, savoring moments of tranquility while the sea breeze carries laughter and the distant calls of seagulls. Fuengirola's beaches are more than just places to soak up the sun; they're sanctuaries of bonding, where families create memories that will be cherished for years to come.

Celebrating Togetherness: The Essence of Fuengirola

Fuengirola's unique blend of relaxation and entertainment is a testament to its celebration of togetherness. It's a place where families can revel in the joy of shared experiences, where parents and children alike can find activities that resonate with their hearts' desires. Whether it's exploring the bustling markets, dancing in the squares, or feeling the sand between their toes, families in Fuengirola are immersed in a sense of belonging that transcends borders and generations.

A Tapestry of Moments to Treasure

In Fuengirola, the boundaries between relaxation and entertainment blur, creating a tapestry of experiences that cater to the multifaceted nature of family life. As the sun sets over the Mediterranean, casting its warm hues across the horizon, families gather to reflect on the day's adventures. The memories created in Fuengirola become a part of their shared narrative, woven into the fabric of their journey together. Fuengirola stands as a testament to the power of simple pleasures, the magic of being present with loved ones, and the art of celebrating life's most precious moments.

3.3.5 Manilva and Casares:

Amidst the well-trodden paths of popular coastal destinations, a world of hidden treasures waits to be discovered by those with an affinity for serenity and seclusion. These lesser-known gems, tucked away from the bustling crowds, unveil a different facet of coastal beauty that resonates with those seeking a quieter, more intimate experience. With unspoiled beaches and an aura of seclusion, these enclaves offer a harmonious escape, where time slows down, and the rhythms of nature take center stage.

Beyond the Beaten Path: The Appeal of Lesser-Known Getaways

The allure of lesser-known coastal getaways lies in their promise of a unique and intimate connection with nature. These hidden corners defy the conventional and beckon the curious traveler to venture beyond the beaten path. Away from the clamor of crowds, the genuine essence of the destination becomes apparent, creating an opportunity for a more personal encounter with its natural beauty and cultural treasures. It's a chance to engage with the environment on a deeper level, to immerse oneself in the tapestry of local life, and to forge a bond with a place that feels like an undiscovered secret.

A Peaceful Retreat: Unveiling Unspoiled Beaches

At the heart of these hidden treasures are the unspoiled beaches that paint a picturesque panorama of tranquility. The sands are untouched by the footprints of many, allowing visitors to claim a slice of paradise for themselves. The gentle murmur of waves serves as a soothing soundtrack, inviting beachgoers to relax, reflect, and rejuvenate. The unspoiled beaches offer a space for quiet contemplation, for solitary walks along the shore, and for forging a connection with the rhythms of the sea that is both profound and deeply personal.

Seclusion and Serenity: The Essence of Hidden Enclaves

In the embrace of these lesser-known getaways, seclusion is not merely a state of being; it's a cherished experience that nurtures the soul. The sense of solitude becomes a gift, allowing travelers to disconnect from the noise of everyday life and find solace in the embrace of nature's wonders. Whether it's watching the sun rise over the horizon in peaceful solitude or stargazing on a secluded beach at night, these hidden enclaves offer moments that remind us of the profound beauty of the world and our place within it.

A Retreat for the Soul: Embracing the Quieter Coastal Experience

The allure of these hidden treasures extends beyond the physical landscape; it resonates with the essence of the human spirit. Those who seek a quieter coastal experience often yearn for a retreat that nurtures the soul. In these secluded corners, the pressures of modern life give way to the simplicity of nature's rhythm. The hushed whispers of wind, the gentle caress of waves, and the rustling of leaves become a symphony of serenity, inviting travelers to reconnect with themselves and with the world in a way that is both profound and restorative.

A Journey of Discovery: Embracing the Unseen

Discovering these hidden coastal getaways is not just an exploration of landscapes; it's a journey of the heart. It's a testament to the beauty that lies beyond what is readily seen, a celebration of the uncharted spaces that offer refuge from the ordinary. These lesser-known gems stand as reminders that amidst the popular destinations, there are still corners of the world waiting to be embraced, places where seclusion, tranquility, and the magic of discovery come together to create an experience that is truly unforgettable.

Whether you're craving the excitement of water sports, the relaxation of beachside lounging, or the exploration of charming villages, the Costa del Sol delivers an enchanting coastal experience that caters to all types of travelers.

CHAPTER FOUR

CULTURAL IMMERSION: FLAMENCO, FESTIVALS, AND GASTRONOMY

4.1 Experiencing the Passionate Art of Flamenco Dancing

Flamenco – a name that resonates with passion, emotion, and the vibrant culture of Andalusia, Spain. Beyond its rhythmic beats and intricate movements, Flamenco is a profound expression of the soul, a dance form that traces its roots deep into the history and heart of the region. When you embark on a journey to Malaga and the Costa del Sol, you're not just visiting a destination; you're entering the realm of Flamenco, where every step, every note, and every gesture tell a story that has endured for centuries.

Flamenco's Origins and Significance:

Flamenco didn't just appear overnight; it's the product of a rich blend of cultures and traditions. It's believed to have emerged from the various cultural influences in Andalusia, including the Roma people, the Moors, and the local Spanish population. Over time, these diverse elements came together to create a unique art form that became the heartbeat of the region.

At its core, Flamenco is more than just a dance – it's a way of expressing profound emotions, ranging from joy and passion to sorrow and longing. The music, the singing, and the dance all come together to create a symphony of sentiment that can resonate deeply within both the performer and the observer.

Experiencing Flamenco:

Witnessing Live Performances:

Imagine stepping into a dimly lit venue, the soft glow of candlelight illuminating the stage. The air is charged with anticipation as the first strains of a guitar begin to play, accompanied by the haunting vocals of a singer. Then, the dancers take the stage, their movements speaking volumes even before they utter a word. From intimate local taverns to grand theaters, Flamenco performances are scattered across Malaga and the Costa del Sol, inviting you to witness the magic firsthand.

The dancers' feet create a rhythmic symphony as they tap and stomp, their dresses twirling and their fingers snapping in perfect harmony. The music pulses through your veins, and you're transported to a place where emotions flow freely, unburdened by words. The experience is visceral, intense, and utterly captivating.

Participating in Workshops:

Have you ever wanted to feel the rhythm of Flamenco under your own feet? Many dance studios and cultural centers in the region offer Flamenco workshops for both beginners and those with some dance experience. Here, you have the chance to learn the basic steps, understand the intricate hand movements, and appreciate the emotional nuances behind each gesture.

As you learn, you'll gain a newfound respect for the artistry and skill that goes into every performance. You'll come to understand that each movement is deliberate, each stomp carries a message, and each sway of the arm conveys a story. Through these workshops, you'll not only learn about Flamenco; you'll become a part of its living legacy.

Flamenco: Beyond the Dance Floor:

Flamenco isn't confined to stages and dance studios; it's woven into the fabric of everyday life in Andalusia. It's in the passionate conversations over a meal, the impromptu gatherings in plazas, and the spirited celebrations that fill the streets. It's a cultural treasure that's passed down from generation to generation, a way of connecting with history, emotion, and one another.

In Conclusion:

Flamenco is a journey – a journey that takes you into the heart of Andalusia, where the music resonates with the rhythm of life itself, and the dance becomes a language of the soul. When you experience Flamenco during your stay in Malaga and the Costa del Sol, you're not just witnessing a performance; you're immersing yourself in a legacy that has endured for centuries. You're connecting with the people, the history, and the spirit of a place that understands the power of expression beyond words.

So, whether you're sitting in the hushed audience of a theater or feeling the beat under your own feet in a dance workshop, let the magic of Flamenco take you on a journey of emotion, rhythm, and culture – a journey that transcends time and space, and leaves an indelible mark on your heart and soul.

4.2 Joining Festivals and Celebrations: Semana Santa and Feria de Malaga

Semana Santa: A Testament to Deep-Rooted Spirituality

In the heart of Andalusia, a profound religious fervor takes center stage during the week leading up to Easter. Semana Santa, or Holy Week, is a time of intense reflection, devotion, and commemoration. Malaga, a city steeped in history and faith, comes alive with a series of processions that weave together faith, culture, and community in a breathtaking display.

The Processions: A Visual and Spiritual Journey

As the sun dips below the horizon, the streets of Malaga are adorned with a sense of reverence and anticipation. Processions of ornate floats, called "pasos," become the focal point of these religious observances. These elaborately crafted floats carry life-sized sculptures depicting scenes from the Passion of Christ and the Virgin Mary. Adorned with intricate details and delicate decorations, each paso is a work of art that has been passed down through generations.

Accompanied by penitents, known as "nazarenos," dressed in traditional robes and conical hoods that obscure their faces, the pasos are carried through the narrow streets with solemn devotion. The hauntingly beautiful sound of saetas – passionate religious songs – fills the air, invoking a sense of spiritual contemplation among the onlookers. The processions create an atmosphere that is both somber and awe-inspiring, as the weight of history and faith converges in a visual and emotional spectacle.

Adorning the Streets: Fragrance and Faith

The streets of Malaga are transformed during Semana Santa. Fragrant flowers, meticulously arranged into intricate patterns called "alfombras," carpet the path of the processions. These floral creations, often combined with colorful sawdust, form a striking contrast against the cobblestones. The alfombras serve as both a symbol of devotion and an offering to the sacred figures that pass over them.

Feria de Malaga: A Celebration of Andalusian Spirit

If your visit to Malaga falls in August, you're in for a vibrant treat – the Feria de Malaga. This week-long extravaganza is a testament to the vivacious spirit and zest for life that defines Andalusian culture. With its origins dating back to the late 15th century, the Feria is a historical celebration that has evolved into a modern fusion of tradition and festivity.

A Kaleidoscope of Colors and Joy

As the sun sets on Malaga, the city undergoes a magical transformation. The streets, adorned with colorful lanterns and banners, come alive with music, dancing, and an infectious energy. The heart of the Feria lies in the "real," a massive fairground on the outskirts of the city. Here, you'll find the iconic casetas – temporary pavilions – where the celebration unfolds.

Casetas: Where Culture and Culinary Delights Meet

The casetas are the heart and soul of the Feria. Each one offers a unique experience, inviting visitors to immerse themselves in the festivities. Step inside to discover a world of lively conversation, traditional music, and energetic dancing. The clinking of glasses and the aroma of local delicacies fill the air, as friends and families gather to celebrate.

A Feast for the Senses: Food, Music, and Dance

Andalusian cuisine takes center stage at the Feria, with stalls and casetas serving up an array of mouthwatering dishes. Indulge in tapas, paella, and an assortment of regional specialties that showcase the rich flavors of the land. As you savor the culinary delights, the lively sounds of flamenco music beckon you to the dance floor. The joyful rhythms and spirited movements are infectious, inviting even the most hesitant to join in the revelry.

Cultural Parades and Fireworks: A Grand Finale

The Feria culminates in a grand parade, where locals don traditional attire, showcasing the vibrant tapestry of Andalusian clothing and culture. The streets become a kaleidoscope of colors, with the joyful procession capturing the essence of the region's rich heritage.

As the week draws to a close, the night sky over Malaga lights up with a spectacular fireworks display, painting the canvas of the city with brilliant bursts of color. The Feria de Malaga is a celebration that transcends time, a spirited testament to the resilient and joyful spirit of Andalusia.

In the Heart of Tradition and Celebration:

Semana Santa and Feria de Malaga are more than mere events on the calendar; they are windows into the soul of Andalusia. Semana Santa invites you to witness the convergence of faith and artistry, to feel the weight of history and devotion in every step of the procession. Feria de Malaga, on the other hand, beckons you to dance, to laugh, and to celebrate the vibrant spirit that defines the region.

Both events are a reflection of the deep-rooted connection between the people of Malaga and their cultural heritage. Whether you find yourself immersed in the solemn beauty of the processions during Semana Santa or swept up in the whirlwind of music, dance, and joy during Feria de Malaga, you'll discover that you're not just a spectator – you're an integral part of these age-old traditions that continue to shape the identity of this enchanting corner of the world.

4.3 Savoring Andalusian Cuisine: Tapas, Seafood, and Traditional Dishes

In the heart of Spain's sunny south, Andalusia is not only known for its stunning landscapes and rich cultural tapestry but also for its extraordinary cuisine. A fusion of flavors that speaks to the region's history, Andalusian gastronomy is a symphony of tastes and aromas influenced by centuries of diverse cultural interactions. From the tantalizing bite-sized tapas to the bounties of the sea, every dish is a celebration of the land's vibrancy and proximity to the Mediterranean. Here's a glimpse into the must-savor delights that await you:

Tantalizing Tapas: The Essence of Sharing

To understand Andalusian dining culture, one must begin with tapas. These delectable small plates aren't just about food; they're about community, camaraderie, and a celebration of flavors. From the simple pleasures of olives and almonds to the more elaborate creations like Iberian ham croquettes and grilled sardines, tapas encapsulate the spirit of sharing and indulgence.

Gazpacho: The Cool Elixir of Summer

Andalusia's warm climate gave birth to one of its most iconic dishes: gazpacho. This chilled tomato-based soup is a refreshing blend of ripe tomatoes, peppers, onions, and cucumbers, often seasoned with olive oil, vinegar, and garlic. Served in tall glasses, gazpacho is a revitalizing way to beat the heat and relish the flavors of the region's fresh produce.

Seafood Sensations: Bounty of the Mediterranean

With its extensive coastline, it's no surprise that Andalusia boasts a cornucopia of seafood delights. From the bustling fish markets to the coastal restaurants, you'll encounter seafood prepared in a myriad of ways, each reflecting the region's culinary prowess. Delight in dishes like "pescaíto frito," an assortment of small, crispy fried fish that offers a flavorful snapshot of life by the sea. For an exquisite treat, don't miss "espeto," skewered sardines grilled over an open flame to perfection, infusing them with a smoky aroma that evokes the essence of the Mediterranean.

Salmorejo: A Creamy Revelation

While often compared to gazpacho, salmorejo is a unique Andalusian creation that deserves its own spotlight. This rich, creamy cold soup hails from Cordoba and is made with tomatoes, bread, olive oil, garlic, and vinegar. The result is a velvety concoction that's often garnished with diced hard-boiled eggs and jamón serrano, creating a harmonious interplay of textures and flavors.

Paella: A Coastal Interpretation

Though not a native dish to Andalusia, paella has become a beloved culinary feature due to the region's proximity to the sea. Seafood paella, a delectable amalgamation of saffron-infused rice and an assortment of fresh seafood, pays homage to the maritime treasures of the Mediterranean. From succulent shrimp to tender calamari, every bite transports you to the shores from which the ingredients were harvested.

A Journey of Flavors and Culture:

Andalusian cuisine is more than just sustenance; it's a reflection of the region's rich history, cultural tapestry, and the rhythms of life. The fusion of flavors echoes the mingling of civilizations that have left their mark on Andalusia throughout the ages. As you savor each bite, you're not just indulging in a meal; you're immersing yourself in the stories of farmers, fishermen, and chefs who have crafted these culinary treasures for generations.

So, when you sit down to enjoy a plate of tapas, savor the cool delight of gazpacho, or relish the ocean's bounty in a seafood feast, remember that you're not just tasting the ingredients – you're tasting the history, the landscapes, and the spirit of Andalusia itself. Through every bite, you're embarking on a journey that takes you beyond the plate, into the heart of a region that expresses its soul through its food.

4.3.1 Recommended Top Restaurants and Their Locations:

When it comes to experiencing the diverse and tantalizing flavors of Andalusian cuisine, a culinary journey through Malaga and its surroundings promises to be an unforgettable adventure. From cozy taverns tucked in historic alleys to elegant waterfront eateries, these top restaurants have earned their reputation for exceptional gastronomy and warm hospitality:

1. El Tintero

Location: Playa del Dedo, 29018 Málaga, Spain

Highlights: El Tintero is not just a restaurant; it's an experience. Set on the beach, this iconic seafood eatery offers a unique dining concept. Servers parade around with freshly caught seafood, and diners bid on their favorites. It's an interactive and lively affair that ensures the freshest catches and a joyful atmosphere.

2. José Carlos García Restaurante

Location: Muelle Uno, Puerto de Málaga, Plaza de la Capilla, 1, 29001 Málaga, Spain

Highlights: With a Michelin star to its name, José Carlos García Restaurante is a culinary haven for those seeking refined dining. Overlooking the marina, the restaurant offers a contemporary take on Andalusian flavors, skillfully crafted by chef José Carlos García.

3. El Pimpi

Location: Calle Granada, 62, 29015 Málaga, Spain

Highlights: El Pimpi is more than a restaurant; it's a living testament to Malaga's history and culture. Set in a historic building, it features a charming courtyard and walls adorned with autographs of famous visitors. Enjoy traditional Andalusian dishes accompanied by an extensive selection of wines.

4. Los Mellizos

Location: Av. Severo Ochoa, 3, 29603 Marbella, Málaga, Spain

Highlights: Los Mellizos is a celebrated seafood restaurant in Marbella, known for its commitment to quality and freshness. Indulge in an array of seafood dishes, from succulent shellfish to expertly grilled fish, all while enjoying views of the Mediterranean.

5. Restaurante Amador

Location: Plaza de la Iglesia, 5, 29670 San Pedro Alcántara, Marbella, Spain

Highlights: Restaurante Amador offers a fusion of traditional and contemporary Andalusian cuisine. Led by chef Mario Cachinero, the restaurant combines local flavors with innovative techniques, resulting in an exceptional dining experience.

6. El Jardín de Lutz at Finca Cortesin

Location: Carretera de Casares, s/n, 29690 Casares, Málaga, Spain

Highlights: Situated within the luxurious Finca Cortesin resort, El Jardín de Lutz offers a refined setting for savoring Andalusian cuisine. The restaurant's enchanting garden terrace provides a picturesque backdrop as you indulge in a menu that celebrates the region's culinary heritage.

7. Restaurante Chinitas

Location: Calle Chinitas, 3, 29015 Málaga, Spain

Highlights: Restaurante Chinitas offers a blend of traditional Andalusian dishes and modern presentations. Located in the heart of Malaga's historic center, it provides a cozy and welcoming atmosphere for experiencing the region's flavors.

8. Restaurante Vino Mío

Location: Calle Vélez Málaga, 5, 29016 Málaga, Spain

Highlights: Restaurante Vino Mío combines innovative culinary concepts with a laid-back ambiance. From creative tapas to elegant main courses, the restaurant offers a diverse range of dishes that showcase the essence of Andalusian cuisine.

9. La Moraga

Location: Plaza de la Merced, 1, 29012 Málaga, Spain

Highlights: La Moraga, with its modern approach to tapas, is a culinary gem in Malaga. Led by Michelin-starred chef Dani García, the restaurant presents a fusion of traditional and avant-garde flavors that appeal to both locals and visitors.

10. Café de Paris

Location: Muelle Ribera, 7, 29660 Marbella, Málaga, Spain

Highlights: Café de Paris, situated along Marbella's marina, offers a blend of French and Mediterranean influences. With stunning sea views, it's a delightful spot to enjoy fresh seafood, succulent steaks, and a touch of European elegance.

Embark on a gastronomic voyage that brings the flavors of Andalusia to your plate, where each restaurant is a gateway to the region's culinary soul. Whether you're seeking traditional tapas, seafood feasts, or innovative interpretations of local classics, these recommended top restaurants promise an exploration of tastes that will leave a lasting impression on your palate.

4.3.2 Recommended Top Nightclubs and Bars and Their Locations:

When the sun sets over Malaga and the Costa del Sol, the region comes alive with a lively nightlife that caters to every taste and preference. From energetic dance floors to stylish cocktail lounges, these top nightclubs and bars offer a diverse range of experiences, ensuring that your evenings are as unforgettable as your days:

1. Sala Gold

Location: Calle Luis de Velázquez, 5, 29008 Málaga, Spain

Highlights: Sala Gold is a dynamic nightclub that pulsates with a mix of electronic and Latin beats. With multiple dance floors, themed parties, and an energetic atmosphere, it's a popular destination for locals and visitors looking to dance the night away.

2. Pangea Club

Location: Muelle Uno, Local 11, Puerto de Málaga, 29016 Málaga, Spain

Highlights: Pangea Club, overlooking the marina, combines sophisticated elegance with a vibrant atmosphere. Known for its stylish interiors, diverse music selection, and outdoor terrace, it's a top choice for those seeking a blend of luxury and entertainment.

3. Sala Trinchera

Location: Calle Parauta, 25, 29006 Málaga, Spain

Highlights: Sala Trinchera is a rock and indie music venue that offers a different kind of nightlife experience. With live concerts, themed parties, and a laid-back ambiance, it's a hub for music enthusiasts and those looking for an alternative atmosphere.

4. Liceo Beach Club

Location: Urbanización Playa, s/n, 29602 Marbella, Málaga, Spain

Highlights: Liceo Beach Club is a glamorous beachfront venue that combines a relaxed beach vibe with sophisticated entertainment. Enjoy cocktails, live DJs, and an upscale beach party experience under the stars.

5. Nikki Beach Marbella

Location: Playa Hotel Don Carlos, Carretera de Cádiz, Km 192, 29604 Marbella, Málaga, Spain

Highlights: Nikki Beach is a global brand known for its upscale beach clubs. In Marbella, you can revel in luxury as you enjoy live music, poolside parties, and a chic atmosphere that epitomizes the glamorous Costa del Sol lifestyle.

6. El Camborio

Location: Plaza de la Merced, 1, 29012 Málaga, Spain

Highlights: El Camborio is a flamenco bar where you can immerse yourself in the passionate rhythms of traditional Spanish music. Enjoy live performances that evoke the spirit of Andalusia, combined with a cozy and intimate setting.

7. La Terraza de la Alcazaba

Location: Calle Alcazabilla, 12, 29015 Málaga, Spain

Highlights: La Terraza de la Alcazaba is a rooftop bar that offers stunning views of Malaga's historic Alcazaba fortress. Sip on cocktails while you take in the city's beauty, creating a perfect blend of relaxation and elegance.

8. Sherry's Corner

Location: Pasaje Nuestra Señora de los Dolores, 13, 29601 Marbella, Málaga, Spain

Highlights: Sherry's Corner is a cozy bar in Marbella known for its warm ambiance and exceptional selection of wines and cocktails. It's an ideal spot for unwinding with friends or enjoying a quiet evening.

9. Bodega El Pimpi

Location: Calle Granada, 62, 29015 Málaga, Spain

Highlights: Bodega El Pimpi, known as a cultural landmark, offers a unique blend of bar and restaurant experiences. Enjoy a glass of wine surrounded by historic décor and live music, immersing yourself in the heart of Malaga's social scene.

10. Karma Beach

Location: Carretera N-340, Km 186, 29600 Marbella, Málaga, Spain

Highlights: Karma Beach is a beach club with a relaxed yet stylish vibe. Nestled on the sandy shores, it offers sun-soaked days and laid-back evenings, making it a perfect destination for beach lovers seeking an enjoyable evening by the sea.

From the beats of electronic music to the soulful sounds of flamenco, the nightlife in Malaga and the Costa del Sol is as diverse as the region itself. Whether you're seeking to dance until dawn, unwind with a cocktail in hand, or soak in the enchanting atmosphere, these recommended top nightclubs and bars promise to infuse your nights with the same magic that defines the region's days.

Indulge in the rich tapestry of Andalusian culture through these experiences, and let the vibrant flavors, captivating rhythms, and warm hospitality of Malaga and the Costa del Sol leave an indelible mark on your travel memories.

CHAPTER FIVE

ARCHITECTURAL WONDERS: MOORISH SPLENDORS AND MODERN MARVELS

5.1 Admiring the Legacy of Moorish Architecture: Alhambra and Nasrid Palaces

The Iberian Peninsula, a crossroads of civilizations and a nexus of cultural interactions, stands as a living testament to the dynamic nature of human history. Within its landscape lies a rich and intricate tapestry of architectural marvels that reflect the ebb and flow of cultures across centuries. Like threads of diverse influences woven together, Spain's architectural heritage showcases the amalgamation of various artistic expressions. One of the most captivating threads in this intricate fabric is the Moorish influence, a legacy that has left an indelible mark on the region's architecture, history, and culture.

A Journey Through Time and Culture: The Alhambra's Enduring Legacy

Nestled amidst the undulating landscapes of Granada, the Alhambra stands as a radiant jewel, glistening with the echoes of history and the intricate craftsmanship of the Moors. A UNESCO World Heritage Site, the Alhambra's significance transcends its role as a mere architectural wonder; it is a testament to the cultural exchanges and influences that have shaped the region. This sprawling palace and fortress complex, dating back to the 13th century, is a testament to the Moorish architectural brilliance that marries aesthetics, functionality, and spirituality.

The Alhambra's grandeur is revealed in every meticulously crafted detail, each element contributing to the symphony of Moorish architecture. The intricate stucco work, a hallmark of this style, adorns the walls like delicate lace, hinting at the dexterity and precision of the artisans who sculpted them. Delicate tile mosaics, reminiscent of a kaleidoscope, form mesmerizing patterns that dance in the sunlight, attesting to the mastery of geometric design. As you traverse the complex's courtyards, an overwhelming sense of tranquility envelops you, drawing you into the serene sanctuary that was once a testament to the Moors' deep connection to nature and spirituality.

The Nasrid Palaces: Opulence and the Fusion of Cultures

At the heart of the Alhambra's enchantment lie the Nasrid Palaces, where opulence and artistic mastery converge. These palaces, adorned with intricate archways, tranquil reflecting pools, and lush gardens, were once the stage upon which the Nasrid dynasty's power and grandeur played out. Stepping into these resplendent halls, visitors are transported through time to an era when Moorish architects crafted spaces that blended the practical with the ethereal. A harmonious marriage of aesthetics and functionality is evident in every alcove, every courtyard, and every archway.

Among the treasures of the Nasrid Palaces, the Palace of the Lions reigns supreme. Its central courtyard, home to the iconic Fountain of Lions, exudes an almost mystical aura that captures the very essence of Islamic architecture and design. This luminous jewel radiates a sense of timelessness, its meticulously carved marble and intricate arches a testament to the architects' unwavering dedication to perfection. Each element, from the water's soothing murmur to the play of light on the surface of the pool, weaves a narrative of beauty, symbolism, and spiritual connection.

The Alhambra: A Portal to the Moorish Era

As visitors step foot within the Alhambra's hallowed halls, they step back in time to a pivotal era marked by the convergence of Islamic, Christian, and Jewish influences. Traces of this multifaceted legacy are etched into the walls, the minarets, and the geometric patterns that adorn every surface. Beyond the sheer aesthetic marvels, the Alhambra encapsulates stories of dynastic shifts, the interplay of cultures, and an unparalleled synthesis of artistic expression that has profoundly shaped the region's history.

Within the Alhambra's walls, the intricate dance of cultural fusion becomes palpable. Islamic aesthetics, with their intricate geometric motifs and stylized calligraphy, seamlessly intertwine with the Christian and Jewish influences that have left their marks on Spain's intricate past. The Alhambra stands as a living embodiment of the Iberian Peninsula's vibrant history, an enduring tribute to the exchange of ideas, aesthetics, and traditions that found its apex in the heart of Andalusia.

An Echo of Bygone Conversations: The Alhambra as a Time Machine

Beneath the sunlight streaming through filigreed windows and the murmur of fountains, visitors are privy to echoes of conversations that once resonated within these walls. Philosophers, artists, and scholars once gathered within these hallowed spaces, engaging in dialogues that shaped the course of history. The Alhambra transcends being a mere physical structure; it is a repository of collective memories, a testament to the shared heritage of humanity. As one wanders through its chambers, it's not just the beauty of Moorish architecture being admired; it's a journey through the corridors of time, bearing witness to the unfolding drama of history itself.

The Alhambra: A Beacon of Cultural Fusion and Architectural Splendor

In closing, the Alhambra stands as an iridescent beacon that illuminates the crossroads of civilizations and underscores the transformative power of architecture. Its legacy endures not solely as an architectural masterpiece but as a living embodiment of the artistic brilliance that flourished during the Moorish era. A visit to the Alhambra and its Nasrid Palaces transcends the role of a typical historical exploration; it becomes an immersive experience, an opportunity to immerse oneself in the intricate tapestry of Spain's past and to profoundly appreciate the enduring influence of the Moors on the country's cultural and architectural heritage. The Alhambra beckons as a symbol of shared human history and a monument to the creative spirit that bridges time and culture.

5.2 Exploring Malaga's Modern Architectural Gems: Pompidou Center and more

Malaga, a city steeped in history and ancient allure, is also a vibrant canvas upon which the strokes of modernity are vividly painted. Amidst the echoes of its rich past, the city has embraced the pulse of the present, fostering a captivating juxtaposition of old and new. At the heart of this evolution stands the Pompidou Center Malaga, a gleaming emblem of contemporary architecture that beckons visitors to explore the city's dynamic cultural scene.

Pompidou Center Malaga: A Multicolored Marvel

The Pompidou Center Malaga stands as a beacon of modernity, an offshoot of its illustrious counterpart in Paris. This architectural gem, characterized by its multicolored cube exterior, stands in striking contrast to the historic tapestry of Malaga's surroundings. This deliberate juxtaposition is more than just an architectural spectacle; it embodies the city's aspiration to embrace the cutting edge while paying homage to its legacy.

The cube, a three-dimensional canvas adorned with bold hues, captures the imagination from afar. It's a declaration of artistic vibrancy, a preview of the vibrant creativity that awaits within. As you step through its doors, you are greeted by a dynamic space that transcends mere gallery walls. The Pompidou Center Malaga is a cultural hub, a space that seamlessly bridges the chasm between tradition and innovation, creating a dialogue between the past and the present.

Artistic Exploration: The Dynamic Space Within

Inside the Pompidou Center Malaga, a realm of modern and contemporary art awaits exploration. The exhibits, a constantly evolving panorama, bring together an eclectic collection of works that challenge conventions and ignite conversations. From avant-garde sculptures to thought-provoking installations, the center's galleries resonate with the pulsating energy of creative expression.

The Pompidou Center Malaga serves as more than just a repository of art; it's a platform for dialogue, a space that invites visitors to ponder, engage, and immerse themselves in the multifaceted narratives woven by artists from around the world. The collision of artistic visions within these walls ignites a spark of inspiration that resonates long after you've departed.

Beyond the Cube: Exploring Malaga's Architectural Marvels

The Pompidou Center is not the sole emissary of Malaga's embrace of modern architectural marvels. The city, with an innate capacity for evolution, boasts an array of other contemporary gems that punctuate its landscape. Among these treasures, the Cube of Contemporary Art, fondly known as "El Cubo," emerges as a symbol of sleek minimalism.

El Cubo, a glass-fronted structure that hosts temporary exhibitions of contemporary artworks, stands as a canvas itself, showcasing the juxtaposition of transparent modernity against the backdrop of traditional surroundings. Its unadorned lines and polished facade create a captivating visual contrast, drawing the eye and inciting curiosity. The interplay of light and transparency serves as an artistic expression in its own right, inviting visitors to engage with the ever-changing exhibits within.

A Modern Oasis: Muelle Uno and Beyond

Venturing beyond the galleries, the city offers a haven of modernity nestled against the azure expanse of the Mediterranean Sea. Muelle Uno, a modern harbor area, marries contemporary architecture with designer boutiques, chic cafes, and waterfront dining. This harbor enclave, pulsating with cosmopolitan energy, stands as a harmonious blend of aesthetics and function, offering an escape from historical echoes and a dive into contemporary sophistication.

Muelle Uno's architecture, characterized by its sleek lines and innovative design, mirrors the reflective surfaces of the sea nearby. Its glass facades seem to merge with the sea's hues, creating an immersive experience that blurs the lines between the urban and the natural. As you stroll along its promenades, you're enveloped in a sensory symphony that evokes the essence of Malaga's dual identity: a city that respects its heritage while embracing the excitement of the present.

A Harmonious Symphony: Past and Present Converge

The modern architectural tapestry of Malaga weaves a narrative that extends beyond individual structures. It's a testament to the city's ability to harmonize its historical past with its contemporary aspirations. Each modern marvel, from the Pompidou Center to El Cubo and Muelle Uno, plays a distinct role in this symphony, contributing a unique note that resonates within the broader composition.

These architectural wonders symbolize more than concrete, glass, and steel; they embody Malaga's evolution into a hub of creativity, innovation, and cultural exchange. They encapsulate the city's invitation to explore, to engage, and to witness the dance of tradition and modernity.

In Conclusion: A Dynamic Dimension to Your Journey

Exploring the modern architectural marvels of Malaga extends your journey beyond the annals of history, immersing you in the city's contemporary spirit. The Pompidou Center, with its vibrant cube exterior and dynamic interior, beckons you to engage with art in new and exciting ways. El Cubo, a haven of minimalism, offers an oasis of contemplation amidst the urban bustle. And Muelle Uno, a testament to urban planning and innovation, invites you to savor the waterfront in style.

As you traverse these architectural wonders, you're not just witnessing the evolution of Malaga; you're experiencing the city's pulse, its heartbeat, and its journey into the future. These modern gems serve as bridges that connect you to the city's creative soul, reminding you that even as time marches forward, the threads of history and innovation remain intricately woven into the fabric of this vibrant Spanish haven.

CHAPTER SIX

NATURAL ESCAPES: MOUNTAINS, CAVES, AND NATIONAL PARKS

6.1 Venturing into the Sierra de las Nieves Natural Park

Nestled amidst the rugged landscapes of the Costa del Sol, the Sierra de las Nieves Natural Park beckons adventurers and nature enthusiasts with its untouched beauty. This protected area is a haven for biodiversity and boasts a diverse range of ecosystems, from lush forests to high-altitude mountain terrain.

Discovering Flora and Fauna

As you embark on your journey through Sierra de las Nieves Natural Park, you'll step into a realm of ecological diversity that thrives in every corner of this enchanting landscape. This protected haven serves as a sanctuary for an impressive array of both flora and fauna, showcasing the resilience of life in its many forms.

A Tapestry of Biodiversity:

From the moment you set foot in Sierra de las Nieves, you'll be surrounded by an intricate tapestry of life. The park's diverse ecosystems offer a perfect balance of habitats that support an incredible variety of plant and animal species. Each step you take reveals a new facet of this natural world, leaving you with a profound appreciation for the intricacies of Earth's ecosystems.

Rare and Endangered Species:

Sierra de las Nieves Natural Park stands as a last refuge for several rare and endangered species that have found solace in its untouched expanses. Among these is the Spanish fir (Abies pinsapo), an ancient coniferous tree species that has managed to survive in only a few isolated pockets in the region. The Spanish fir's elegant branches stretch toward the sky, an emblem of endurance in the face of changing landscapes.

Another remarkable resident of the park is the Spanish ibex (Capra pyrenaica hispanica), often referred to as the symbol of the mountainous regions of Andalusia. This agile and majestic mammal navigates the rocky terrain with grace, its impressive curved horns serving as a testament to its resilience in the face of adversity.

Symphony of Avian Life:

For avid birdwatchers, Sierra de las Nieves is nothing short of a paradise. The air comes alive with the calls, songs, and flights of numerous avian species that have found their niche within the park's varied habitats. Raptors soar overhead, their keen eyes searching for prey. Vibrant songbirds perch on branches, filling the air with melodious tunes that echo through the trees.

As you traverse the trails, you might catch sight of the Griffon vulture, its impressive wingspan a marvel as it rides thermal currents high above the landscape. The chittering calls of the European goldfinch provide a cheerful soundtrack to your exploration, while the secretive Eurasian scops owl might reveal itself under the cover of twilight.

An Invitation to Understanding:

Sierra de las Nieves Natural Park offers not just a physical journey but an intellectual and emotional one as well. Exploring this rich tapestry of life encourages us to reflect on the interconnectedness of all living things and the importance of preserving these delicate ecosystems. As you immerse yourself in the diverse flora and fauna, you'll come to understand the invaluable role that protected areas like this one play in maintaining the world's ecological balance.

In Sierra de las Nieves, the rustle of leaves, the call of a distant bird, and the scent of wildflowers combine to create an experience that touches all your senses, leaving you with a lasting impression of the wonders that thrive in this secluded corner of the Costa del Sol.

The Enchanted Forests

Within the embrace of Sierra de las Nieves Natural Park, a realm of enchantment awaits as you delve into its captivating forests. These verdant havens are not mere collections of trees; they are living, breathing tapestries of life that have flourished for centuries, forming a sanctuary for both nature enthusiasts and those seeking solace in the embrace of unspoiled beauty.

A Verdant Oasis:

Stepping into the enchanting forests of Sierra de las Nieves is like entering a world of perpetual green. The dense vegetation forms a lush carpet that stretches as far as the eye can see. Towering trees, their trunks adorned with moss and ferns, create a canopy that filters sunlight into dappled patterns, casting a gentle glow upon the forest floor.

The Symphony of Water:

As you venture deeper into this botanical sanctuary, the symphony of water greets your ears. Trickling streams meander through the undergrowth, their soothing melodies intertwining with the chorus of birdsong that fills the air. The streams converge to form miniature cascades and waterfalls, their crystalline waters carving their path through the landscape, shaping rocks into sculptures of fluid grace.

Spanish Fir Forest: A Living Relic:

One of the most cherished aspects of these forests is the presence of the Spanish fir (Abies pinsapo), a tree species that has defied the passage of time. Standing tall and regal, these ancient conifers harken back to an era long before human footprints left their mark. The Spanish firs create a cathedral-like atmosphere, their branches reaching upward as if in eternal worship of the sky.

Wildflower Tapestry:

Spring is a season of pure enchantment within these forests. As the snow of winter recedes, it gives way to a vibrant tapestry of wildflowers that burst forth from the forest floor. Delicate blossoms of vivid hues—violets, blues, reds, and yellows—carpet the ground, turning the landscape into a living canvas of color. These blossoms dance in harmony with the gentle breeze, infusing the air with a sweet and delicate fragrance.

A Portrait of Timelessness:

Exploring these forests is akin to embarking on a journey through time. The verdant beauty you witness has remained largely unchanged for centuries, a testament to the enduring power of nature to shape and sustain life. Whether you're an avid botanist, an aspiring painter, or simply someone seeking a tranquil escape, these enchanting forests offer a glimpse into a world untouched by the rapid pace of modern life.

Amidst the rustling leaves and the filtered sunlight, you'll find a profound sense of connection to the natural world and an appreciation for the intricate beauty that surrounds us. Sierra de las Nieves' enchanting forests invite you to pause, to breathe, and to immerse yourself in the timeless embrace of nature's wonders.

Peaks and Panoramas

Embarking on the ascent to the pinnacle of Sierra de las Nieves, the renowned Pico Torrecilla, is an adventure that promises not only physical exertion but also an unparalleled reward that transcends the boundaries of the senses. This lofty summit, standing as a sentinel over the surrounding landscape, beckons adventurers and explorers to embrace the challenge and witness nature's grandeur on an awe-inspiring scale.

Ascending to the Sky:

The journey to Pico Torrecilla is a tale of elevation, a narrative where each step brings you closer to the heavens. As you make your way along the well-trodden path, your senses heighten with the crispness of the air and the rhythmic percussion of your footsteps against the earth. The ascent is a rhythmic dance, a harmonious fusion of physical effort and the symphony of nature's sounds—birdsong, the rustle of leaves, and the distant hum of the wind.

Conquering the Summit:

With each successive step, the world around you transforms. Trees give way to shrubs, and the trail begins to reveal sweeping views of the landscape below. As you approach the summit of Pico Torrecilla, a palpable sense of anticipation builds—a promise of the breathtaking vista that awaits you. The final push, though challenging, is propelled by the allure of the panoramic reward.

A Spectacle of Splendor:

And then, you stand atop Pico Torrecilla. The panoramic spectacle that unfolds before you is nothing short of a masterpiece painted by nature itself. The rolling hills stretch out like the waves of an undulating sea, their emerald hues merging seamlessly with the azure of the Mediterranean horizon. The sun's gentle caress casts a warm glow, illuminating the landscape and accentuating its contours and textures.

A Glimpse of Infinity:

From this vantage point, your perspective shifts. You're no longer a mere observer; you've become a part of the landscape, an integral thread woven into the fabric of nature's artistry. The horizon stretches infinitely, a testament to the boundless expanse of the world. Gazing upon this vista, you're reminded of the profound beauty and complexity of our planet, an intricate tapestry that extends far beyond what the eye can see.

A Soulful Connection:

As you stand on the summit of Pico Torrecilla, surrounded by the vastness of the world below, you realize that this moment is more than just a visual spectacle—it's a profound connection. The energy of the earth courses through your veins, and a sense of serenity envelops your being. Amidst the silence, you hear the whispers of generations that have treaded these paths before you, paying homage to the same view that now captures your imagination.

Venturing to Pico Torrecilla isn't just a hike; it's an odyssey of the spirit, a communion with nature's grandeur, and a reminder of the intricate beauty that exists both within and beyond us. This summit, reached through sweat, determination, and a touch of wonder, leaves an indelible mark on your heart and soul, inspiring you to cherish the beauty of the natural world and the boundless heights that the human spirit can attain.

6.2 Unearthing the Wonders of Nerja's Caves and Cliffs

Hidden beneath the town of Nerja lies a subterranean wonderland that captivates visitors from around the world. The Nerja Caves, also known as Cuevas de Nerja, are a testament to the intricate beauty of nature's geological artistry.

Stalactites and Stalagmites

Embarking on a journey into the heart of Nerja's Caves is akin to stepping through a portal into another world—a world sculpted by the patient hands of time and nature's creative forces. As you venture deeper into the caverns, the realm you encounter is one of sheer wonder, where the artistry of geological processes is on full display, and where the very essence of time seems to stand still.

A Subterranean Masterpiece:

As you cross the threshold into the cave's interior, the air changes, carrying with it a sense of anticipation and curiosity. The cavern's ceilings reach towering heights, adorned with formations that defy imagination. Stalactites, like delicate crystal chandeliers, hang from above, the result of countless drops of mineral-rich water that have sculpted these formations over eons. Below, stalagmites rise from the floor, reaching upward as if in a slow-motion dance with their ceiling-bound counterparts.

The Echoes of Millennia:

Walking through the cave's chambers, you're transported through the annals of time itself. The formations you encounter have been meticulously shaped over thousands of years, each droplet of water leaving behind a trace of itself in the mineral deposits it carries. It's a reminder that, while we may measure time in human terms, nature has its own, more patient rhythm—a rhythm that leaves an indelible mark on the landscape.

A Play of Light and Shadow:

As you navigate the intricate pathways of the caverns, the interplay between light and shadow takes center stage. Illuminated by carefully placed lights, the formations come alive with an ethereal glow. The stark contrast between the darkness and the illuminated structures creates an almost mystical atmosphere. Shadows dance upon the walls, lending an air of enchantment to the subterranean landscape.

An Intimate Encounter:

The caves' interiors have a way of inspiring reverence—an appreciation for the quiet beauty that emerges when nature's forces align. Standing amidst these ancient formations, you become part of the tableau, a witness to the ceaseless dance of mineral-rich water and stone. The cool air, the faint echoes of dripping water, and the sense of history etched into the walls converge to create an intimate encounter with the Earth's geological narrative.

A Glimpse into Deep Time:

Stepping into Nerja's Caves is more than a mere exploration; it's a connection to the passage of time and the natural forces that have shaped the world around us. The stalactites and stalagmites, formed drop by drop, remind us of the extraordinary beauty that emerges when the ordinary processes of nature are given the canvas of millennia. This subterranean landscape holds secrets written in stone, inviting you to become a part of its story, if only for a fleeting moment.

The Concert Hall: An Underground Marvel

In the heart of the Nerja Caves lies a chamber that defies the boundaries of both nature and art—a place where the ancient rhythms of the Earth harmonize with the melodies of human creativity. This chamber, known as the Concert Hall, is a testament to the extraordinary acoustics that the Earth's own architecture can bestow upon a space. It's not just a geological formation; it's a living testament to the marriage of nature's elegance and the human spirit's boundless ingenuity.

The Grand Stage of the Earth:

Upon stepping into the Concert Hall, you're immediately greeted by its vast expanse. The ceiling arches above, forming a natural dome that dwarfs the audience below. The walls, adorned with intricate formations that have taken millennia to evolve, provide a backdrop of unparalleled beauty. It's as if you're standing within a cathedral—except this cathedral is sculpted entirely by the Earth itself.

Acoustics That Echo through Time:

As whispers of sound grace the air, the true magic of the Concert Hall emerges. The acoustics of this space are nothing short of extraordinary. Every note sung, every chord played, resonates with a depth and clarity that transcends the norm. Sounds cascade off the walls and reverberate through the chamber, creating an enveloping cocoon of sonic perfection.

Nature's Symphony:

It's not difficult to imagine why the Concert Hall has served as the venue for a myriad of musical performances and cultural events. The marriage of astounding acoustics and the exquisite beauty of the surroundings creates an ambiance that is both awe-inspiring and intimate. Whether it's the haunting strains of a cello, the lilting notes of a flute, or the resounding timbre of a vocal ensemble, every sound finds its place in this natural amphitheater.

A Fusion of Nature and Art:

The convergence of music and nature within the Concert Hall is a testament to humanity's ability to find harmony within the world around us. The very act of performing music within these walls feels like a tribute to the Earth's symphony—an acknowledgment that the rhythms of nature are woven into the fabric of our creative expressions. It's a moment when human endeavor becomes a seamless part of the grander narrative of the planet.

A Tribute to the Sublime:

The Concert Hall in the Nerja Caves is more than just a venue; it's a testament to the transcendent beauty that exists at the juncture of human aspiration and nature's gifts. As music resonates through the air and the formations glisten in the soft light, it's a reminder that art has the power to elevate, just as the Earth itself can elevate our understanding of beauty and possibility. In this sacred space, past and present merge, creating a symphony that echoes through both the chambers of the cave and the chambers of the human heart.

Ancient Artifacts and History

Beneath the surface beauty of the Nerja Caves lies a treasure trove that transcends time itself—an archaeological tapestry that unveils the stories of those who walked the Earth long before us. As you delve into the depths of these ancient chambers, you're not just surrounded by the impressive geological formations; you're immersed in a history that spans millennia, offering a window into the lives, cultures, and struggles of prehistoric humans who once inhabited this awe-inspiring realm.

A Journey Through Time:

Walking amidst the stalactites and stalagmites, your gaze is drawn not only upwards and downwards but also inward—towards the layers of history that the cave's walls have absorbed over countless generations. The very rocks bear witness to the passage of time, holding within them the echoes of footsteps, the warmth of fires, and the stories of lives long past.

The Artifacts of Ancients:

The Nerja Caves have yielded a wealth of artifacts that tell tales of humanity's distant past. Implements of daily life—tools, pottery, and decorative objects—have been meticulously preserved by the cave's unique environment. These items provide insights into the technologies, aesthetics, and perhaps even the beliefs of ancient societies that once thrived in the region.

The Artistry of the Ancients:

Among the most striking discoveries within the caves are the prehistoric paintings that grace the walls. These ancient artworks, created using natural pigments, depict scenes of daily life, animals, and symbolic forms. The flickering light of torches and fires would have danced upon these walls, casting the art in a warm, almost magical glow.

A Glimpse into Daily Life:

As you explore the remnants of ancient civilizations within the Nerja Caves, you're given a unique opportunity to connect with the people who left their mark upon the cave's history. The tools they used, the art they created, and the objects they cherished become tangible links to a world that existed long before written history. You begin to see the threads that connect their experiences to our own, recognizing the universality of human curiosity, creativity, and the pursuit of meaning.

A Reminder of Our Ancestry:

The archaeological wonders of the Nerja Caves remind us that our stories are eternally intertwined with those who have come before us. These artifacts, lovingly preserved by the Earth's embrace, serve as a bridge between past and present—a reminder that the legacies of ancient civilizations continue to resonate in the cultural tapestry of today's world.

Stepping through time within the Nerja Caves is a humbling experience, an acknowledgement that our brief lives are just a part of a grander narrative that has been unfolding for thousands of years. Amidst the formations that nature has crafted and the artifacts that human hands have shaped, you find a connection not only to the past but also to the shared journey of humanity—an exploration of existence that transcends the boundaries of time and space.

6.3 Hiking the Majestic Mountains and Enjoying Breathtaking Views

For those who seek adventure and a connection with nature, the Costa del Sol offers a plethora of hiking opportunities that lead to unforgettable vistas. Whether you're a seasoned hiker or a casual explorer, the region's majestic mountains offer trails suited to all levels of experience.

The Challenge of El Caminito del Rey

For the intrepid souls seeking an exhilarating adventure amidst the raw forces of nature, El Caminito del Rey beckons as a daring challenge and a testament to both human ingenuity and the majestic power of the environment. This renowned trail, renowned as "The King's Little Pathway," is not merely a hike; it's a heart-pounding journey that traverses the precipitous walls of a steep gorge, offering an adrenaline-infused encounter with vertiginous heights and breathtaking vistas.

A Glimpse of the Extraordinary:

Setting foot onto El Caminito del Rey is like embarking on a pilgrimage to the edge of the possible. The trail is aptly named, as it clings to the side of the cliffs like a fragile thread, defying gravity with a boldness that makes every step an act of courage. As you navigate the narrow path suspended above the void, the world below becomes a mosaic of color and contour—a canvas that only the brave and the curious dare to tread.

The Power of Perspective:

As you traverse El Caminito del Rey, the views it unveils are nothing short of breathtaking. The Guadalhorce River, like a silvery serpent, winds its way through the valley below, carving a path amidst the rugged terrain. From your precarious vantage point, you gain a newfound appreciation for the scale and grandeur of the landscape—an intimate communion with the sheer magnitude of the natural world.

A Dance with Adrenaline:

The heart races as you negotiate narrow walkways and steel suspension bridges that seem to sway gently with the breeze. Each step is a daring proclamation of your determination to embrace the unknown, to explore the limits of your comfort zone, and to bask in the thrill of confronting your fears head-on. The exhilaration of knowing that you're walking where only the boldest venture is a rush that heightens every sense.

Nature's Grand Spectacle:

While the trail's thrilling nature captivates the adventurous spirit, the journey also celebrates the unadulterated beauty of the surroundings. The stark contrast between the rugged cliffs and the azure sky serves as a backdrop for a symphony of colors and textures that ebb and flow with the passing light. The songs of birds, the rustle of leaves, and the distant echoes of the river below create an orchestral arrangement that accompanies your every step.

A Testimony to Bravery:

El Caminito del Rey is not just a trail; it's a testimony to the indomitable spirit of human exploration. With each careful step, you become a part of the trail's history—a history that harkens back to its construction in the early 20th century and that has been woven with tales of adventure and wonder. Conquering this pathway is a celebration of human courage, a tribute to the connection between the daring and the beauty that thrives in the wild.

As you emerge from El Caminito del Rey, heart still pounding from the adventure, you carry with you more than just the memory of an extraordinary hike. You carry a sense of accomplishment, a newfound respect for the power of nature, and the realization that the boundaries of human potential can be extended when we dare to challenge the edges of our own comfort.

Trails of Varied Beauty

The hiking trails that weave their way through the landscapes of the Costa del Sol are a testament to the region's diverse natural beauty, offering a tapestry of experiences that cater to every kind of explorer. Whether you're an avid outdoors enthusiast, a nature lover, or simply seeking a respite from the ordinary, these trails serve as a gateway to a world of discovery, wonder, and personal challenge.

Coastal Adventures:

For those who find solace in the rhythmic lapping of waves against the shore, the coastal trails along the Costa del Sol provide a symphony of sea breezes, panoramic horizons, and the tranquil allure of the Mediterranean. Wander along well-maintained paths that hug the coastline, allowing the gentle caress of the sea air to soothe your senses. Every step unveils a new view, whether it's a secluded cove, a charming fishing village, or the endless expanse of the azure sea.

Mountain Retreats:

Elevate your adventure by venturing into the embrace of the Costa del Sol's majestic mountains. Here, the trails lead you through ancient woodlands, where the scent of pine fills the air and the whisper of leaves accompanies your journey. Ascend through landscapes that change with the altitude—woodlands giving way to rocky vistas, and rocky vistas yielding to sweeping panoramas. With every ascent, you'll leave the ordinary behind and forge a connection with the raw beauty of the Earth.

Varied Terrain for All:

The beauty of the Costa del Sol's hiking trails lies in their adaptability. Whether you're traveling with family, friends, or embarking on a solo expedition, the options are as varied as the desires of the hiker. Leisurely strolls along well-marked paths are perfect for families, providing opportunities for exploration without straining young legs. Intermediate treks offer a balance of challenge and reward, while seasoned hikers will find their mettle tested on strenuous routes that lead to heights where the reward is nothing short of breathtaking.

Nature's Classroom:

As you traverse these diverse landscapes, you're not just wandering; you're immersing yourself in a living classroom of nature's wonders. Enthusiastic birdwatchers can spot avian inhabitants darting through trees, while botany enthusiasts can marvel at the variety of flora that thrives in each ecosystem. The quiet moments of solitude offer introspection, while group hikes become occasions for camaraderie and shared memories.

The Gift of Choice:

The hiking trails of the Costa del Sol don't merely offer paths; they offer choices. The choice to meander along the coast or ascend into the mountains. The choice to challenge yourself or enjoy a leisurely stroll. The choice to connect with nature, to experience its wonders firsthand, and to find a rhythm that resonates with your heart's desires.

Amidst the Costa del Sol's diverse trails, you're given the gift of choice—to choose your pace, your path, and your connection with the world around you. With every step, you're not just traversing a trail; you're exploring a spectrum of experiences, embracing the beauty of the natural world, and crafting a personal narrative within the grand tapestry of the Costa del Sol's landscapes.

Nature's Rewards at the Summit

The trails that lead intrepid hikers to the summits of the Costa del Sol's peaks are not just pathways—they're gateways to perspectives that redefine your understanding of the world around you. The ascent, though demanding, is a labor of love—a commitment to exploration and a tribute to the boundless beauty that waits at the journey's culmination. With every step, you're investing not just in physical effort but in an experience that is woven into the very fabric of your being.

A Symphony of Scenery:

As you ascend the steep trails, your anticipation grows—an anticipation for what lies beyond the horizon, an eagerness to witness the world from an elevated vantage point. And when you finally stand atop the summit, your breath is stolen by the symphony of scenery that unfolds before you. It's a crescendo of natural artistry—the sprawling coastline of the Mediterranean Sea, kissed by the sun's golden embrace, stretches to the horizon. The valleys below are adorned with a quilt of verdant hues, and the distant peaks create a dramatic backdrop that etches itself into your memory.

Coastline Serenades:

For those who have conquered the coastal trails, the rewards are nothing short of enchanting. Gazing out at the sparkling waters of the Mediterranean Sea, you become one with the rhythm of the tides, your heart echoing the waves that crash against the shore. The coastline, seen from this elevated perspective, appears both fragile and infinite—a reminder of the delicate balance that nature weaves into every corner of the Earth.

Valleys of Tranquility:

The lush valleys that stretch out below summon you to peer into their depths—a kaleidoscope of greens, browns, and occasional bursts of vibrant color. It's a world teeming with life, where the interplay of light and shadow creates a dynamic canvas that evolves with the passing of the sun.

Here, amidst the valleys, you find a tranquil retreat—a place where the whispers of the wind become a melody that soothes the soul.

Peaks of Majesty:

The towering peaks, crowned by the sky and often shrouded in mist, instill a sense of humility. They remind you that nature's grandeur extends beyond the realms of human accomplishment, and that the mountains are guardians of ancient secrets. Standing upon these summits, you feel a connection to generations past, a connection that transcends time and speaks to the infinite cycles of life that have played out beneath these very skies.

A World of Discovery:

Every trail, every ascent, holds the promise of discovery—a discovery that is not just visual, but visceral. It's a discovery of the vastness of the Earth and the boundless wonder that resides within it. As you soak in the panoramas, you're gifted with a new perspective—a perspective that broadens your understanding of the interconnectedness of all things and ignites a fire within to protect and preserve the natural splendor that has unfurled itself before you.

In conquering these trails, you're not just reaching a summit; you're reaching a heightened sense of awareness, a profound connection to the world, and an intimate understanding of the awe-inspiring beauty that graces the Costa del Sol. Each panoramic vista becomes a memory etched into your soul—a reminder that the world is vast, that your place in it is both unique and interconnected, and that the pursuit of exploration is an eternal journey that both humbles and uplifts the human spirit.

CHAPTER SEVEN

LEISURE AND ENTERTAINMENT

7.1 Embracing Nightlife in Malaga and Coastal Hotspots

When the sun sets over Malaga and the Costa del Sol, the vibrant nightlife comes to life, offering an array of entertainment options for every taste. From chic bars overlooking the Mediterranean to pulsating nightclubs where the music never stops, the region offers a diverse and lively nightlife scene.

Beachfront Bars and Clubs: A Riveting Nightlife by the Sea

Malaga's enchanting coastline boasts not only pristine beaches and azure waters but also a thriving nightlife that takes the notion of beachside entertainment to the next level. As the sun's golden rays dip below the horizon, the atmosphere along the shoreline transforms into a lively and electrifying scene, offering an array of beach clubs and bars that cater to those seeking both relaxation and revelry.

Beach Parties That Come Alive: The allure of beach parties is undeniable, and Malaga's beachfront bars and clubs know exactly how to bring this allure to life. These venues set the stage for unforgettable nights where the rhythmic crash of waves serves as the backdrop for music, dance, and celebration. The feel of soft sand beneath your feet and the salty sea breeze in the air add a unique touch of enchantment to the festivities. It's an immersive experience that connects you to both the vivacity of the night and the soothing presence of the sea.

Live Music Under the Stars: As night descends upon Malaga, the beach clubs come alive with the sounds of live music that resonate through the night air. From soulful acoustic performances to energetic bands playing the latest hits, the musical offerings cater to diverse tastes. The sound of guitars strumming, drums beating, and voices soaring under the starlit sky creates an atmosphere that's simultaneously intimate and communal.

DJ Sets that Ignite the Night: For those who seek to dance the night away, the DJ sets at these beachfront establishments are nothing short of exhilarating. Expertly curated playlists span genres, ensuring that every track pulses with energy and rhythm. The music isn't confined to a single genre; instead, it evolves as the night progresses, seamlessly transitioning from laid-back tunes as the sun sets to high-energy beats that keep the dance floor alive until dawn. The pulsating lights, the contagious energy of the crowd, and the ethereal beauty of the sea create an electric ambiance that's bound to keep you moving.

Old Town Ambiance: Where History Meets Nightlife

As darkness blankets the city, the historic heart of Malaga takes on a new persona, offering a beguiling juxtaposition of ancient architecture and modern merriment. The old town's narrow, winding alleys and charming squares, which may have been peaceful and reflective during the day, metamorphose into bustling meeting points that beckon visitors to explore the nightlife that the city has to offer.

Tapas Bars that Spill Onto the Streets: One of the most immersive ways to experience Malaga's nightlife is by partaking in the beloved tradition of tapas. The old town is home to a myriad of tapas bars, many of which spill out onto the cobblestone streets. This creates an atmosphere that's as inviting as it is vibrant – imagine sitting under the soft glow of street lamps, sharing small plates of delectable local fare, and engaging in lively conversations with fellow patrons.

A Sensory Journey of Flavors: The tapas culture in Malaga is not just about the food; it's an experience that engages all your senses. The rich aromas of grilled meats, the harmonious clinking of glasses, and the lively chatter of patrons all contribute to the sensory tapestry of the night. Each tapa tells a story – a story of tradition, of innovation, and of the region's culinary identity. From succulent grilled sardines to melt-in-your-mouth Iberian ham, the variety and quality of tapas offerings reflect the depth of Malaga's gastronomic heritage.

Mingling with Locals and Travelers: The old town's magnetic pull brings together locals and visitors, creating a blend of cultures and backgrounds that's reflective of Malaga's open and welcoming spirit. The narrow streets become conduits for interaction, as people from all walks of life converge to enjoy the offerings of the night. It's a unique opportunity to engage in conversations with locals, sharing stories, insights, and laughter over shared plates and glasses of local wine.

Marbella's Glamorous Nightlife: A World of Opulence

Known as a playground for the wealthy and glamorous, Marbella's nightlife scene is a reflection of the town's luxurious reputation. The nightlife in Marbella is not just about entertainment; it's about indulgence, exclusivity, and a glimpse into a world of opulence that's truly unique to this coastal gem.

Puerto Banús: The Epitome of Luxury: At the heart of Marbella's nightlife is Puerto Banús, a marina that exudes extravagance. This exclusive enclave is lined with high-end boutiques, upscale restaurants, and, of course, glamorous bars and clubs. As the night sets in, Puerto Banús transforms into a hub of energy and sophistication, where you can revel in the company of international jet-setters, celebrities, and those who simply appreciate the finer things in life.

Upscale Bars and Clubs: The bars and clubs in Marbella are designed to cater to those with a taste for luxury. These establishments aren't just places to enjoy drinks and music; they're immersive experiences that transport you to a realm of elegance and indulgence. From exquisitely crafted cocktails to top-tier service, every detail is carefully curated to create an ambiance that resonates with the town's glamorous reputation.

The Allure of Celestial Views: One of the defining features of Marbella's nightlife is the stunning views that many of its establishments offer. Imagine sipping champagne under the moonlight while overlooking the glimmering sea or enjoying cocktails on a rooftop terrace that offers panoramic vistas of the Mediterranean. These celestial views add an element of enchantment to the already captivating nightlife experience.

In conclusion, the nightlife of Malaga and the Costa del Sol is a tapestry woven with diverse threads, each contributing to a vibrant and unforgettable experience. Whether you're dancing the night away on the shores, exploring the historical charm of the old town after dark, or indulging in the opulent world of Marbella's glamorous scene, the nights in this region offer something for everyone. The magic of the night, combined with the backdrop of the sea and the warmth of the Mediterranean culture, creates an atmosphere that's simultaneously exhilarating and inviting – a true testament to the enchanting charms of Malaga and the Costa del Sol.

7.2 Shopping, Markets, and Local Handicrafts: Where to Find the Best Souvenirs

Bringing back a piece of the Malaga and Costa del Sol experience with you is a delightful way to preserve your memories. The region offers a variety of shopping opportunities, from bustling markets to boutique stores, where you can find unique souvenirs and local crafts.

Exploring Local Treasures: Shopping Experiences in Malaga and Marbella

When it comes to shopping, Malaga and Marbella are destinations that cater to a wide range of tastes and preferences. From historic markets brimming with local flavors to charming craft markets that celebrate artisanal craftsmanship, and from high-end designer boutiques to quaint local shops, the shopping experiences in these regions are as diverse as the landscapes that surround them.

Mercado Central de Atarazanas: A Culinary Haven and Cultural Gem

Located in the heart of Malaga, the Mercado Central de Atarazanas stands as a testament to the city's rich history and vibrant present. This historic market, nestled within an architectural marvel that dates back to the 14th century, is not merely a place to shop; it's an immersive experience that encapsulates the essence of Andalusia's culinary and cultural heritage.

An Abundance of Freshness: As you step into the market's bustling interior, your senses are immediately engaged by the symphony of colors, aromas, and sounds that envelop you. Stalls laden with the freshest produce, from plump tomatoes to luscious fruits, showcase the region's bountiful agricultural offerings. The selection of meats, seafood, and cured ham is a testament to the culinary traditions that have been cherished for generations.

Indulge in Local Flavors: The Mercado Central de Atarazanas is not just a market; it's a gateway to experiencing the authentic flavors of Andalusia. Here, you'll find an array of local products that are synonymous with the region's gastronomic identity. Sample and purchase artisanal cheeses, delectable olive oils, and wines that have been crafted with a dedication to preserving traditions. Engaging with the vendors and hearing their stories adds a personal touch to your shopping experience.

Rediscovering Tradition: The market's location within a historic shipyard (atarazanas in Spanish) lends an air of heritage and significance to your shopping journey. The intricate stained glass window that serves as its centerpiece is a nod to the market's history, inviting you to pause and appreciate the fusion of tradition and modernity that defines Malaga's spirit.

Craft Markets: Embracing Artisanal Excellence

Beyond the mainstream shopping hubs, a dynamic and vibrant craft scene thrives in the heart of Malaga and its coastal towns. Craft markets, which dot the city and its surroundings, offer an opportunity to connect with local artisans and uncover unique creations that encapsulate the region's creative soul.

Artistry in Every Corner: The craft markets that intermittently appear across the city and the coastal towns bring together a diverse community of artisans. From jewelry designers who weave stories into intricate pieces to ceramic artists who infuse their work with Mediterranean aesthetics, the markets are a melting pot of creativity. Each booth tells a story of passion, skill, and a deep connection to the local culture.

Meaningful Keepsakes: The items you find in these craft markets are more than mere objects; they're a reflection of the artist's dedication to their craft and a celebration of individuality. Whether you're seeking a hand-painted ceramic piece to adorn your home, a unique piece of jewelry that captures the essence of the sea, or textiles that exude the warmth of Andalusia, each purchase becomes a meaningful keepsake that carries a piece of the region with it.

An Invitation to Interact: One of the joys of exploring craft markets is the opportunity to interact with the creators themselves. Engaging in conversations with the artisans provides insight into their creative process, the inspirations behind their work, and the stories that shape their pieces. These interactions transform your shopping experience into a personal journey of discovery and connection.

Marbella's Shopping Promenade: Where Elegance Meets Retail Therapy

In Marbella, shopping is not just an activity; it's an experience that mirrors the town's reputation for luxury and refinement. The shopping promenade that stretches along the coast is a true embodiment of this ethos, offering a blend of high-end designer boutiques, well-known brands, and local shops that create an enticing tapestry of retail therapy.

Elegance by the Sea: The setting itself is an integral part of the shopping experience in Marbella. As you walk along the promenade, the gentle caress of the sea breeze and the panoramic views of the Mediterranean provide a serene backdrop to your shopping excursion. The seamless integration of nature and shopping creates an atmosphere that's both relaxing and invigorating.

Designer Destinations: For those seeking the crème de la crème of fashion and luxury, Marbella's shopping promenade doesn't disappoint. International designer boutiques line the streets, showcasing the latest trends and timeless classics. From haute couture dresses to exquisite accessories, the offerings cater to those with a penchant for elegance and sophistication.

Local Flavors and Boutiques: Amidst the designer showcases, you'll also find charming local shops that celebrate the essence of Marbella's culture and creativity. These boutiques offer a curated selection of artisanal products, unique fashion pieces, and handcrafted jewelry that capture the spirit of the region. Exploring these hidden gems adds a touch of authenticity to your shopping experience.

In the end, shopping in Malaga and Marbella is not merely about acquiring material possessions; it's about immersing yourself in the tapestry of the region's culture, history, and craftsmanship. Whether you're exploring the vibrant Mercado Central de Atarazanas, engaging with artisans at craft markets, or indulging in retail therapy along Marbella's promenade, each experience is an opportunity to connect with the heart and soul of these enchanting destinations.

7.3 Enjoying Family-Friendly Activities and Amusement Parks

Malaga and the Costa del Sol aren't just for adults; they also offer a plethora of family-friendly activities and amusement parks that cater to visitors of all ages.

Unforgettable Family Adventures in Malaga and the Costa del Sol

Malaga and the Costa del Sol aren't just destinations for adults seeking history, culture, and nightlife; they're also havens for families in search of unforgettable experiences that cater to every age. From thrilling amusement parks to immersive wildlife encounters and the endless possibilities of beachside fun, the region offers a plethora of family-friendly activities that ensure everyone in your group has a fantastic time.

Tivoli World: A Wonderland for All Ages

Nestled in the charming town of Benalmádena, Tivoli World stands as a beacon of joy and excitement for families seeking a day of wholesome fun. This amusement park isn't just a collection of rides; it's a world where dreams come true and smiles are the order of the day.

Endless Entertainment: The heart of Tivoli World beats with an assortment of rides that cater to every level of thrill-seeker. From heart-pounding roller coasters that twist and turn through the air to gentle carousels that bring smiles to the faces of the little ones, the range of attractions ensures that there's something for everyone. As the laughter of children and the excited shouts of adventurers fill the air, the park comes alive with a sense of joy and camaraderie.

Themed Areas for All: Tivoli World understands the diverse needs of families, which is why it features themed areas that cater to various age groups. While older children and teenagers might find themselves drawn to the adrenaline-fueled rides, younger visitors can explore enchanting areas that are tailor-made for their interests. From whimsical fantasy lands to charming rides that evoke a sense of nostalgia, Tivoli World crafts an experience that's immersive and engaging for everyone.

A Day of Memories: As you navigate through Tivoli World, you'll find not just rides, but also live shows, entertainers, and food stalls that elevate the experience. The park's atmosphere is vibrant and infectious, encouraging families to come together, share moments of exhilaration, and create cherished memories that will last a lifetime.

Bioparc Fuengirola: A Journey into the Wild

For families with a fascination for wildlife and a desire to connect with nature, Bioparc Fuengirola is a haven that offers an experience like no other. This innovative zoo has redefined the concept of animal exhibits, creating environments that closely mimic the animals' natural habitats and allowing visitors to witness the magic of wildlife up close.

An Immersive Experience: As you step into Bioparc Fuengirola, you're immediately transported into a world of lush vegetation, meandering streams, and captivating landscapes. The design of the zoo ensures that animals roam freely in environments that reflect their native homes, providing an immersive experience that educates and delights visitors of all ages. Whether it's watching a group of lemurs leap from branch to branch or observing a family of gorillas interact, each encounter is a testament to the zoo's commitment to conservation and animal welfare.

Learning Through Discovery: Bioparc Fuengirola goes beyond entertainment; it's a space of learning and discovery. Through guided tours, informative displays, and interactive experiences, families can deepen their understanding of wildlife conservation and the intricate ecosystems that support these magnificent creatures. The zoo's dedication to education empowers younger generations to become stewards of the environment and advocates for the preservation of endangered species.

Awe and Wonder: For children, the zoo is a place of wonder and awe. Watching animals in their natural environments instills a sense of respect for the world's biodiversity and a curiosity about the natural world. From the playful antics of meerkats to the graceful movements of big cats, every moment at Bioparc Fuengirola is an opportunity for families to connect with the animal kingdom and develop a deeper appreciation for the delicate balance of life on Earth.

Beach Adventures: Where Every Moment is a Treasure

The Costa del Sol's golden beaches are iconic, but their appeal isn't limited to sunbathing alone. Families can make the most of these breathtaking coastlines by engaging in a variety of beachside activities that cater to every member's preferences.

Water Sports and Thrills: For families seeking adventure, the region's beaches offer an array of water sports that promise adrenaline rushes and unforgettable moments. Whether it's windsurfing, kayaking, paddleboarding, or jet skiing, the calm waters of the Mediterranean provide the perfect playground for aquatic fun. Experienced instructors and rental facilities ensure that everyone, from beginners to experts, can participate in these exciting activities.

Creative Sandcastle Building: The simple pleasure of building sandcastles isn't confined to children alone; it's an activity that invites families to tap into their creativity and imagination. Spend quality time together constructing intricate fortresses, sprawling cities, or whimsical sculptures that defy the bounds of your creativity. These sandcastle-building sessions are not just about the end result; they're about fostering bonds, nurturing teamwork, and creating memories that stand the test of time.

Leisurely Strolls and Picnics: Sometimes, the most memorable moments are the ones that unfold at a leisurely pace. Take a leisurely stroll along the shoreline, feeling the soft sand beneath your feet and the gentle caress of the sea breeze on your skin. Set up a cozy picnic with your family, savoring the simple joys of fresh fruit, sandwiches, and laughter against the backdrop of the vast blue expanse.

In essence, Malaga and the Costa del Sol offer families an invitation to embark on journeys of joy, discovery, and connection. Whether it's the exhilaration of Tivoli World's rides, the wonder of Bioparc Fuengirola's wildlife, or the endless possibilities of beachside adventures, each experience is a testament to the region's commitment to ensuring that every member of the family finds their own piece of paradise. Through these shared moments of excitement, education, and relaxation, families are bound to create memories that will be cherished for generations to come.

Whether you're seeking an energetic night out, hunting for the perfect souvenir, or planning a family adventure, Malaga and the Costa del Sol have a diverse range of experiences to offer.

CHAPTER EIGHT
ACCOMMODATION OPTION
8.1 Luxury Resorts and Villas

When you find yourself yearning for a journey of pure indulgence and unadulterated relaxation, the captivating realm of Malaga and the Costa del Sol stands ready to welcome you with open arms. This sun-kissed haven is not just a destination; it's a realm of luxury that redefines the very essence of opulence and lavishness.

Looming on the horizon are a selection of extravagant resorts and exclusive private villas, each poised to immerse you in a world of grandeur and serenity. These are not mere accommodations; they are sanctuaries of refined living where every detail is meticulously crafted to cater to your desires. Immerse yourself in a realm of unparalleled service, where your every whim is anticipated and met with a gracious smile.

Gaze upon stunning landscapes that stretch to the horizon, each one a canvas of nature's artistry. Perched upon cliff edges or nestled amid lush gardens, these havens offer breathtaking views that capture the essence of the Mediterranean's azure embrace. Step onto your private terrace or balcony and witness the sun casting its golden hues upon the waves, turning them into molten gold.

The amenities offered within these paradisiacal retreats are not just mere conveniences; they are lavish expressions of hospitality. Infinity pools seemingly merge with the ocean, creating an illusion of swimming into eternity. Lounges adorned with plush furnishings invite you to surrender to leisure, while world-class spas beckon with promises of rejuvenation. Here, tradition meets innovation as ancient Moorish rituals inspire spa treatments that transport you to realms of pure bliss.

As the sun dips below the horizon, the magic continues to unfold. Savor the exquisite flavors of the region, expertly prepared by culinary artisans who fuse traditional recipes with modern sophistication. Dine beneath the stars, the sound of lapping waves serenading you as you embark on a gastronomic journey through Andalusia's rich culinary heritage.

These resorts are not just places to stay; they are experiences to be savored. They are an embodiment of the desire for the extraordinary, the pursuit of perfection in every facet of your journey. From the impeccable service that surpasses expectation to the meticulously appointed suites that cocoon you in comfort, every moment spent within these walls is a symphony of luxury.

In the embrace of the Malaga and Costa del Sol's luxurious retreats, you'll find yourself transported to a realm where time slows, where the worries of the world are cast aside, and where the art of relaxation is elevated to its highest form. This is not just a getaway; it's a transcendent experience that lingers in your memories long after you've left its shores—a testament to the unbridled allure of this enchanting destination.

8.1.1 Recommended Top Luxury Resorts And Villas With Their Locations

Here are some of the top luxury resorts and villas in the Malaga and Costa del Sol region, along with their locations:

Marbella Club Hotel, Golf Resort & Spa

Location: Marbella

Description: An iconic resort blending timeless elegance with modern luxury, offering a private beach, golf courses, and a renowned spa.

Puente Romano Marbella

Location: Marbella

Description: A Mediterranean village-style resort featuring lush gardens, beachfront access, Michelin-starred dining, and world-class tennis facilities.

Finca Cortesin Hotel Golf & Spa

Location: Casares

Description: A secluded retreat offering a championship golf course, lavish spa, and impeccable service amid a picturesque Andalusian setting.

Villa Padierna Palace Hotel

Location: Benahavís

Description: A palatial resort known for its elegant architecture, three golf courses, Roman-style spa, and breathtaking views of the coast.

Anantara Villa Padierna Palace Benahavís Marbella Resort

Location: Benahavís

Description: A luxurious oasis featuring elegant accommodations, a tranquil spa, and panoramic views of the Mediterranean Sea.

Hotel Don Pepe Gran Meliá

Location: Marbella

Description: A beachfront gem offering lavish suites, lush gardens, and a renowned restaurant overlooking the sea.

Casa La Concha Boutique Hotel

Location: Marbella

Description: An intimate boutique hotel nestled in the hills, offering stunning views, personalized service, and an aura of tranquility.

Villa Cullinan Marbella

Location: Marbella

Description: An exquisite private villa with luxurious amenities, infinity pool, and captivating vistas of the Mediterranean coastline.

Villa Picasso

Location: Mijas

Description: A lavish villa featuring a private pool, panoramic sea views, and easy access to the beaches and attractions of Mijas.

Villa Malaga Sunset

Location: Malaga

Description: A contemporary villa with infinity pool, spacious interiors, and awe-inspiring sunsets over the Mediterranean.

Villa El Paraíso

Location: Estepona

Description: A stunning villa boasting modern design, private pool, and proximity to golf courses and beaches.

Villa Azure

Location: Nerja

Description: A luxurious villa with sleek design, infinity pool, and panoramic vistas of Nerja's coastline.

These luxury resorts and villas are meticulously designed to provide the utmost comfort, impeccable service, and breathtaking surroundings, ensuring an unforgettable stay in the enchanting Malaga and Costa del Sol region.

8.2 Boutique Hotels and Charming Inns

If your heart yearns for an experience that transcends the ordinary and craves the embrace of accommodations as unique as your own spirit, then boutique hotels and charming inns await to enfold you in their unmatched allure. These are not just places to rest your head; they are veritable havens of character, stories, and connections that are waiting to be discovered.

Tucked away in historic edifices and nestled in the secret folds of the city, these establishments offer a glimpse into the past, each one a living embodiment of a bygone era. Wander down cobbled streets and find yourself standing before these hidden gems, where the walls themselves seem to whisper tales of ages long past. It's as if these buildings have witnessed the unfolding of history and are now inviting you to be a part of their narrative.

Step through the doors and into a realm where personalized attention is not just a service; it's a way of life. The staff are not just attendants; they are storytellers, eager to share the hidden gems of the city, recommend the best local eateries, and ensure that your every need is met with genuine warmth. Here, your stay is not simply a transaction; it's a connection forged between kindred spirits who share a love for the extraordinary.

In these enclaves of charm, the notion of "one size fits all" is left at the door. Instead, you'll find interiors that reflect the very essence of the locale, each design element carefully chosen to pay homage to the city's heritage. Whether it's exposed beams and rustic furnishings that evoke the spirit of Andalusia or contemporary art pieces that add a touch of modern flair, every corner is a testament to the artistry of the surroundings.

Often, these establishments embrace themes that transport you to worlds beyond the ordinary. From nautical-themed inns that evoke the romance of the sea to art-inspired retreats that ignite your creative spirit, each boutique stay is a canvas of imagination where you are not just a guest but a participant in a carefully curated experience.

As the sun sets over the charming streets, return to your sanctuary of serenity. Sink into plush beds adorned with the finest linens, feeling the weight of the world lift as you surrender to comfort. Awake refreshed, knowing that a delectable breakfast awaits—each bite a culinary masterpiece that fuels your explorations of the city that lies just beyond your doorstep.

These boutique hotels and inns are not just accommodations; they are gateways to a world that beckons with open arms. They are invitations to immerse yourself in the culture, the stories, and the magic of Malaga and the Costa del Sol. So, step inside, embrace the unique, and let yourself be enchanted by the charms that these carefully crafted spaces have to offer.

8.2.1 Recommended Top Boutique Hotels and Charming Inns With Their Locations

Here are some of the top boutique hotels and charming inns in the Malaga and Costa del Sol region, along with their locations:

Hotel Claude Marbella

Location: Marbella

Description: A luxurious boutique hotel set in a 17th-century mansion, offering elegant rooms, a tranquil courtyard, and personalized service.

Hotel Palacio Blanco

Location: Vélez-Málaga

Description: A charming inn in a restored 18th-century palace, featuring uniquely decorated rooms, a rooftop terrace, and a central location.

La Villa Marbella

Location: Marbella

Description: An intimate and romantic boutique hotel with Moroccan-inspired decor, lush gardens, and a cozy atmosphere.

La Fonda Hotel

Location: Benalmádena

Description: A quaint and historic inn with a central location, offering individually designed rooms, traditional Andalusian architecture, and a rooftop pool.

Hotel Casa 1800

Location: Málaga

Description: A hidden gem with a blend of classic and contemporary design, offering cozy rooms, a central courtyard, and a rooftop terrace.

La Posada del Ángel

Location: Ojén

Description: A rustic yet elegant inn set in a charming village, providing stunning views, rustic decor, and a peaceful ambiance.

Hotel El Pintón de Júlia

Location: Frigiliana

Description: A boutique hotel nestled in the heart of a white-washed village, offering cozy rooms, a lovely garden, and a warm, welcoming atmosphere.

La Morada Mas Hermosa

Location: Málaga

Description: A quirky and artistic boutique hotel with individually designed rooms, an art gallery, and a rooftop terrace.

La Posada Morisca

Location: Almuñécar

Description: A charming inn inspired by Moorish architecture, offering stunning sea views, cozy rooms, and a peaceful garden.

Hotel Claude Urban

Location: Marbella

Description: A contemporary urban retreat with stylish rooms, modern design, and a central location near the Old Town.

El Oceano Beach Hotel

Location: Mijas Costa

Description: A beachfront boutique hotel featuring luxury suites, a beach club, and breathtaking views of the Mediterranean.

Hotel Molino del Santo

Location: Benaoján

Description: A rustic-chic inn set in a former olive mill, surrounded by stunning natural landscapes and offering a restaurant with local cuisine.

These boutique hotels and charming inns capture the essence of the region's history, culture, and beauty, providing a personalized and immersive experience for travelers seeking something truly exceptional.

8.3 Cozy Beachfront B&Bs

Close your eyes and picture this: as the first light of dawn gently paints the sky with shades of pink and gold, you stir from your slumber to the tranquil symphony of waves rhythmically caressing the shore. The gentle sounds of the sea become the backdrop to your awakening, a soothing lullaby that welcomes you to a new day in paradise. The invigorating scent of the salty sea breeze wafts through the open windows, carrying with it the promise of adventures yet to unfold.

Such enchanting mornings are the hallmark of the cozy beachfront bed and breakfasts that grace the Costa del Sol. Nestled just steps away from the sandy embrace of the coastline, these hidden gems offer more than just a place to rest your head. They are intimate havens where you can immerse yourself in the region's natural splendor, awakening your senses to the magic of the Mediterranean.

Imagine stepping onto your private terrace, a cup of freshly brewed coffee in hand, as the sun inches higher in the sky, casting a warm and inviting glow over the world. The soft sand stretches out before you, a canvas of possibilities where you can choose to bask in the sun's embrace or take a leisurely morning stroll along the water's edge. Each footstep carries you closer to the heart of this coastal paradise, a destination that beckons you to explore and discover its treasures.

Cozy beachfront bed and breakfasts embody a range of styles that reflect the diverse personalities of their guests. Some exude a rustic charm, with weathered wooden beams and furnishings that evoke a sense of history and nostalgia. Others boast a contemporary elegance, where sleek lines and modern design elements complement the natural beauty that surrounds them. What they all share is a commitment to providing you with an authentic and unforgettable experience.

Whether you're seeking a romantic escape with your loved one or a peaceful retreat to rejuvenate your spirit, these

B&Bs offer a slice of paradise tailored to your desires. The symphony of the sea will serenade you to sleep each night, and the gentle embrace of the ocean will greet you anew each morning. Each day is a canvas, waiting for you to fill it with exploration, relaxation, and cherished memories.

So, as you imagine waking up to the gentle sounds of waves and the invigorating sea breeze, know that this dream can become a reality on the sun-kissed shores of the Costa del Sol. Cozy beachfront bed and breakfasts await to envelop you in their embrace, offering you the chance to experience nature's beauty in its purest form and create moments that will forever hold a special place in your heart.

8.3.1 Recommended Top Cozy Beachfront B&Bs With Their Locations

Here are some of the top cozy beachfront bed and breakfasts in the Malaga and Costa del Sol region, along with their locations:

La Luna Blanca Beach Resort

Location: Estepona

Description: A charming beachfront B&B offering cozy rooms, direct access to the beach, and stunning views of the Mediterranean.

Casa La Concha Boutique Hotel

Location: Marbella

Description: An intimate B&B nestled in the hills, offering breathtaking sea views, personalized service, and a tranquil atmosphere.

El Lodge Ski & Spa

Location: Sierra Nevada

Description: A cozy mountain B&B offering ski-in/ski-out access, spa facilities, and rustic-chic accommodations.

Hostal La Posada

Location: Nerja

Description: A beachfront B&B with a laid-back atmosphere, comfortable rooms, and a central location near Nerja's attractions.

Hotel La Casa del Califa

Location: Vejer de la Frontera

Description: A unique B&B set in a historic building, offering characterful rooms, a rooftop terrace, and easy access to the beach.

Playa Los Arcos

Location: Maro, Nerja

Description: A beachfront B&B with a relaxed vibe, offering simple yet comfortable accommodations and direct access to Playa de Maro.

Casa Garcia Boutique Bed & Breakfast

Location: Benalmádena

Description: A charming B&B with sea views, cozy rooms, and a welcoming atmosphere near the beach.

Casa Veracruz

Location: Marbella

Description: An intimate B&B with Andalusian charm, offering a courtyard garden, comfortable rooms, and a short walk to the beach.

El Encanto Inn

Location: Rincón de la Victoria

Description: A beachfront B&B with a cozy ambiance, offering sea-view rooms, a sun terrace, and a serene location.

Casa SiempreViva

Location: Mijas

Description: A rustic B&B with stunning sea views, comfortable rooms, and a peaceful garden setting.

Hostal Restaurante Playa Azul

Location: Torre del Mar

Description: A family-run B&B right on the beach, offering affordable rooms, a restaurant, and a friendly atmosphere.

Beach Hostel La Plata

Location: Benalmádena

Description: A budget-friendly beachfront B&B with a relaxed vibe, communal spaces, and direct access to the beach.

These cozy beachfront bed and breakfasts offer a chance to experience the tranquility and beauty of the Costa del Sol's shores, providing a warm and inviting atmosphere for travelers seeking a serene escape by the sea.

8.4 Hostels and Guest Houses

For those whose hearts beat to the rhythm of wanderlust and adventure, the array of hostels and guest houses that dot the landscape of Malaga and its coastal fringes offer a gateway to a world of possibilities. Whether you're driven by a budget-conscious spirit or a yearning for vibrant camaraderie, these accommodations beckon with open arms, promising an experience that transcends mere lodgings.

Imagine stepping into the heart of a bustling hostel, where travelers from all corners of the globe converge to share their stories and forge connections that span continents. The air is electric with the anticipation of new friendships, as the clinking of glasses and the hum of laughter fill the communal spaces. Here, the world is your oyster, and the bonds you form become the pearls that enrich your journey.

These budget-friendly havens are designed with the modern traveler in mind, understanding that comfort and community are paramount. The dorm-style rooms are not just spaces to rest; they're realms where dreams take shape, as adventurers swap tales of their escapades and collaborate on future exploits. Colorful murals and vibrant decor infuse the spaces with a sense of vitality, reflecting the energy of the travelers who call these places home, if only for a while.

As you find yourself in the heart of the action, you'll notice that these hostels and guest houses are more than just accommodations. They are hubs of social interaction, where communal kitchens become culinary laboratories where international flavors blend, and common areas transform into theaters of cultural exchange where languages and traditions converge.

Budget-conscious travel doesn't mean sacrificing comfort. Many of these accommodations offer well-equipped kitchens where you can prepare your own meals, saving both money and the opportunity to savor local ingredients. The convenience of on-site amenities, from laundry facilities to cozy lounges, ensures that you have all you need at your fingertips, allowing you to focus your resources on exploring the wonders of the region.

But beyond the practicalities, it's the sense of unity that truly sets these establishments apart. You'll find yourself among kindred spirits, united by a shared love for exploration and discovery. Whether you're embarking on a sunrise hike or heading out to explore the vibrant nightlife, the connections you've forged within these walls become your companions, your allies, and your fellow adventurers.

So, whether you're a budget-savvy traveler seeking economical accommodations or an enthusiastic explorer eager to embrace the world, these hostels and guest houses offer an invitation to be a part of a global community. They are more than just places to stay; they're gateways to unforgettable experiences, where your journey is enriched by the people you meet and the stories you share.

8.4.1 Recommended Top Hostels and Guest Houses With Their Locations

Here are some of the top hostels and guest houses in the Malaga and Costa del Sol region, along with their locations:

The Lights Hostel

Location: Malaga

Description: A trendy and social hostel located in the heart of Malaga's Old Town, offering stylish dorms and a vibrant atmosphere.

Oasis Backpackers' Hostel Malaga

Location: Malaga

Description: A lively hostel with a rooftop terrace and bar, providing comfortable dorms and a central location.

Alcazaba Premium Hostel

Location: Malaga

Description: A modern and chic hostel set within a historic building, offering stylish rooms and a rooftop bar with panoramic views.

Picnic Dreams Boutique Hostel

Location: Malaga

Description: A boutique-style hostel with artistic decor, cozy common areas, and a central location near attractions.

Nomad Hostel

Location: Malaga

Description: A welcoming and social hostel with a laid-back atmosphere, offering comfortable dorms and a communal kitchen.

Feel Hostels Soho Malaga

Location: Malaga

Description: A hip hostel with a creative vibe, situated in the artsy Soho district and offering a rooftop terrace.

Los Amigos Beach Hostel

Location: Torremolinos

Description: A beachfront hostel with a vibrant atmosphere, offering direct access to the beach and social events.

La Palma Hostel

Location: Marbella

Description: A cozy and friendly hostel with a relaxed vibe, offering comfortable rooms and a central location.

Casa Al Sur Terraza Hostel

Location: Malaga

Description: A laid-back hostel with a rooftop terrace, offering dorms and private rooms, and a focus on community.

El Nómada Hostel

Location: Nerja

Description: A boutique-style hostel with a tranquil garden and social spaces, providing a comfortable retreat near the beach.

Hostel Bellavista Playa

Location: Marbella

Description: A budget-friendly hostel with a beachfront location, offering a lively atmosphere and sea views.

Aloha Pueblo Hostel

Location: Marbella

Description: A unique and relaxed hostel in a picturesque village, offering comfortable rooms and easy access to the coast.

These hostels and guest houses provide a range of options for budget-conscious travelers and those seeking a vibrant social atmosphere, making it easy to connect with fellow adventurers while exploring the beauty of the Costa del Sol.

8.5 Best Neighborhoods to Stay
In the realm of travel, the choice of where to lay your hat isn't just a logistical decision; it's a gateway to a unique world

waiting to be explored. The neighborhoods you choose to call home during your sojourn can shape your experience, coloring your days with distinctive hues and textures. This realization holds true in the Malaga and Costa del Sol region, where each neighborhood is a microcosm of culture, history, and allure.

As you embark on your journey, the timeless streets of Malaga's Old Town invite you to step back in time. Here, the echoes of history are woven into the cobblestones, and the facades of centuries-old buildings whisper tales of eras long past. The ambiance is one of enchantment, with narrow alleys leading to hidden plazas adorned with fountains and flowers. Immerse yourself in the rhythm of daily life as locals go about their business, and stumble upon the birthplace of Picasso, a testament to the city's artistic heritage.

For those who crave a touch of sophistication and luxury, the allure of Marbella's Golden Mile is irresistible. This stretch of opulence and glamour is where celebrities and jet-setters converge, enjoying designer boutiques, upscale restaurants, and lavish beach clubs. The Mediterranean glitters like a jewel in the sun, and the seafront promenade becomes a stage for fashionable strolls and people-watching. The Golden Mile is an embodiment of indulgence, a realm where elegance meets the shimmering sea.

Venture further and discover the charm of Mijas, a village perched on the hills overlooking the coast. This whitewashed haven is a visual delight, its streets adorned with colorful flower pots and panoramic vistas of the Mediterranean. The tranquility is palpable, and as you navigate its winding alleys, you'll encounter artists' studios, quaint cafes, and a sense of serenity that beckons you to slow down and savor the moment.

But if your heart beats to the rhythm of the night, then Benalmádena's lively marina is your stage. Neon lights dance upon the water's surface, and the air is alive with the sounds of laughter and music. Restaurants, bars, and clubs beckon with promises of vibrant nightlife, and the energy is infectious as revelers come together to celebrate life.

The right neighborhood isn't just a backdrop; it's an integral part of your journey. It's a canvas that you paint with your experiences, a portal through which you'll weave the stories that will remain etched in memory. Whether your heart resonates with cultural exploration, beachfront living, or vibrant nightlife, the Malaga and Costa del Sol region offers a tapestry of neighborhoods, each offering its own unique allure. So, choose wisely, and embark on an adventure that will be colored by the ambiance of your chosen corner of paradise.

8.6 Local Apps for Booking Accommodation

In the modern age of travel, technology has made booking accommodations easier and more convenient than ever. Here are some local apps for booking accommodation in the Malaga and Costa del Sol region:

ByHours: This app specializes in microstays, allowing you to book hotel rooms for a few hours rather than a full day. This can be particularly useful for layovers, business trips, or short stays along the coast.

Badi: While not exclusively for accommodations, Badi is a platform for finding roommates and shared apartments. If you're planning an extended stay in the region, this app can help you connect with locals for shared housing.

WaytoStay: This app focuses on vacation rentals and apartment bookings. It offers a range of options for those who prefer the comfort and convenience of a home away from home while exploring the Costa del Sol.

Niumba: This app is part of TripAdvisor and offers a variety of vacation rentals, apartments, and holiday homes across the region. It's a great choice for travelers seeking a homey atmosphere during their stay.

Only-apartments: As the name suggests, this app is dedicated to apartment rentals. It provides a wide selection of apartments in various neighborhoods, giving you a chance to live like a local during your visit.

Apartool: If you're interested in serviced apartments and aparthotels, Apartool is a useful app. It offers a range of accommodations with amenities that make your stay comfortable and convenient.

Apartamentos Fuengirola Playa: This local app specializes in vacation rentals and apartments in Fuengirola, a popular coastal town in the Costa del Sol. It's a good choice for those looking to explore this specific area.

Costa del Sol Rentals: Focusing on vacation rentals and holiday homes along the Costa del Sol, this app provides options for accommodations that suit different preferences and budgets.

Apartamentos Málaga: If you're looking for apartments in Malaga, this app is worth considering. It offers a selection of apartments in various parts of the city, giving you a chance to experience local life.

Mijas Rentals and Sales: For those interested in Mijas, this app specializes in vacation rentals and real estate options in and around this charming village.

These local apps offer a range of options for booking accommodations in the Malaga and Costa del Sol region, catering to different preferences and travel styles. Always ensure to read reviews and do thorough research before making a booking to ensure a pleasant stay.

CHAPTER NINE

Day Trips and Beyond

9.1 Exploring Ronda: A Town on the Edge of the Cliff

Perched dramatically on the edge of a deep gorge, Ronda is a picturesque town that captures the essence of Andalusia's rugged beauty. Its breathtaking location, straddling the El Tajo gorge, has bestowed upon it a unique and mesmerizing identity that has solidified its position as one of the most iconic destinations in the region. As the sun's golden rays cast their enchanting glow upon the town, Ronda's sheer cliffs and historic structures seem to come alive with history and charm.

Ronda's rich history dates back to ancient times, and its landscape is a testament to the passage of ages. The town bears traces of its Roman and Moorish heritage, their influences interwoven into its very fabric. The remnants of these civilizations can be seen in the architecture, the layout of the streets, and the culture that pervades the town. Ronda's history is a narrative of resilience, adaptation, and continuity.

But it's Ronda's remarkable geographical setting that truly sets it apart. Perched precipitously on the edge of the El Tajo gorge, the town's vantage point offers visitors a truly awe-inspiring experience. As you approach Ronda, the sight of the Puente Nuevo (New Bridge) spanning the gorge is nothing short of breathtaking. This architectural marvel, a feat accomplished in the 18th century, symbolizes Ronda's determination to overcome its challenging natural surroundings. The bridge serves not only as a link between the newer and older parts of the town but also as a portal to panoramic vistas that defy imagination. From its towering arches, one can behold the grandeur of the rugged cliffs, the winding path of the Guadalevín River carving its way through the gorge below, and the verdant landscapes that stretch out in all directions.

Exploring Ronda's Old Town is akin to stepping through a time portal. Cobblestone streets wind like ancient pathways, leading curious wanderers through the heart of the town. The charming white-washed houses, adorned with colorful flowerpots, exude an air of nostalgia. Each step reveals quaint doorways, hidden plazas, and architectural details that hint at centuries past. This well-preserved tapestry of the past envelops visitors in a sense of wonder and reverence for the history that lives on in every stone.

At the core of Ronda's Old Town lies the Plaza de España, a vibrant central square that serves as a nexus of life in the town. Encircled by cafes, restaurants, and shops, the plaza is an invitation to experience the rhythm of daily existence in Ronda. The shade of age-old trees offers respite from the sun's warmth, while the chatter of locals and the laughter of visitors create a symphony of human interaction. The square becomes an epicenter of communal life, where stories are shared, friendships are forged, and the pulse of the town is felt most vividly.

Yet, the heart of Ronda beats not only in its plazas but also in its traditions. The town's historic bullring, the Plaza de Toros de Ronda, stands as a testament to a cultural legacy that has withstood the test of time. One of the oldest bullrings in Spain, it echoes with the memories of countless events that have unfolded within its sandstone walls. This connection to the art of bullfighting is deeply intertwined with Ronda's cultural identity, reflecting the town's historical roots.

The grandeur of the arena, with its graceful sandstone arches and its circular layout, evokes a sense of timelessness. Upon crossing the threshold, one can almost feel the energy of past events reverberating through the air, carried by the whispers of history. The Plaza de Toros doesn't merely exist as an architectural marvel; it's a living testament to a tradition that has shaped the town's soul.

However, the story of Ronda's bullring extends beyond its physical structure. Within its walls, an engaging museum unfolds, inviting visitors to delve into the multifaceted world of bullfighting. This curated space takes guests on a journey through time, charting the evolution of the tradition, its significance within Spanish society, and the artistic nuances that define each encounter in the ring. Exhibits range from historical artifacts that trace the history of bullfighting to intricate costumes that evoke the pageantry of the arena. The museum is a window into the essence of this art form, offering insights that transcend mere spectacle.

In conclusion, Ronda's allure is an intricate tapestry woven from its breathtaking landscape, architectural marvels, and the echoes of history that resonate throughout its streets. The town's ability to seamlessly blend its rich heritage with its natural surroundings is a testament to the enduring charm of Andalusia's landscapes and culture. Ronda beckons travelers to embark on a journey into the past, to marvel at the ingenuity of architectural feats, and to embrace the heart of a town that stands as a bridge between eras and experiences. As the sun sets behind the cliffs, casting an ethereal glow over the town, Ronda's story continues to unfold, a narrative etched into the very fabric of time and place.

9.2 Journeying to Granada: Alhambra and Albaicín District

Granada, a city that conjures visions of Moorish grandeur and artistic brilliance, is a must-visit destination when exploring Andalusia. Nestled against the backdrop of the majestic Sierra Nevada mountains, this enchanting city is a treasure trove of history, culture, and architectural wonders. From its humble beginnings as a Moorish stronghold to its current status as a vibrant cultural hub, Granada's allure is irresistible to travelers seeking a blend of rich heritage and modern vibrancy.

The crown jewel of Granada is undoubtedly the Alhambra, a UNESCO World Heritage Site that stands as an epitome of the city's historical significance and architectural excellence. This sprawling palace complex is a living testament to centuries of cultural fusion, a masterpiece that seamlessly integrates Islamic, Christian, and Renaissance influences. The Alhambra's Nasrid Palaces, characterized by their meticulously carved stucco, intricate tilework, and serene courtyards, showcase the pinnacle of Islamic architectural achievement. The Palacio de Comares and the Palacio de los Leones stand as awe-inspiring examples of the delicate interplay between form and function, aesthetics and spirituality.

Within the Alhambra complex, the Generalife Gardens offer a serene retreat from the bustling world outside. These meticulously designed landscapes are a testament to the harmonious coexistence between nature and human creativity. Meandering pathways lead to tranquil courtyards adorned with fountains that emanate the soothing sound of flowing water. The scent of blooming flowers lingers in the air, creating an atmosphere of quiet contemplation. The Generalife is more than a garden; it's a place where history, art, and nature converge to create an experience that resonates with the soul.

Venture into the Albaicín district, a labyrinth of narrow streets and white-washed houses that narrate the city's Moorish legacy. Stepping into the Albaicín is like entering a time capsule that transports you to the era when Granada was a flourishing Moorish capital. The district's architecture, layout, and atmosphere all reflect the Moorish influence that has left an indelible mark on the city. As you wander through the winding alleys, you'll encounter hidden plazas, quaint patios, and ornate doorways that whisper tales of centuries past.

The Mirador de San Nicolás stands as a pinnacle vantage point within the Albaicín, offering a panoramic view of the Alhambra against the backdrop of the Sierra Nevada mountains. As the sun sets and bathes the palace complex in warm hues, the view is nothing short of magical. It's a moment that encapsulates the essence of Granada's beauty, where history, nature, and human achievement converge to create an unforgettable sight.

But Granada's allure doesn't stop at its architecture and vistas; it extends to its culinary and cultural offerings. The Albaicín district comes alive with the sounds of flamenco music that echo through its narrow streets. The passionate rhythms, heartfelt melodies, and expressive dances of flamenco convey the depth of Andalusian culture and emotion. Alongside the music, the aroma of traditional Andalusian dishes fills the air. Tapas bars and local eateries invite you to savor delights like gazpacho, tortilla española, and paella, each dish a symphony of flavors that pay homage to the region's culinary heritage.

In conclusion, Granada stands as a testament to the power of history, art, and human creativity to shape a city's identity. From the resplendent Alhambra that embodies centuries of cultural fusion to the winding streets of the Albaicín that whisper tales of the past, every corner of Granada tells a story. A visit to this city is not merely a journey through time; it's an immersive experience that evokes a sense of wonder, a connection to the past, and an appreciation for the beauty that arises when cultures collide and coexist. Granada is more than a destination; it's an exploration of the intricate tapestry that weaves together human history and creativity.

9.3 Venturing into the Historic City of Cordoba

Cordoba, once a cultural and intellectual epicenter of the medieval world, exudes a unique charm that weaves together its rich history of Moorish, Christian, and Jewish influences.

With every step you take through its labyrinthine streets, you're treading on the footprints of civilizations that have left an indelible mark on the city's identity. Cordoba stands as a living testament to the dynamic interplay of cultures and religions that have shaped its character.

The highlight of Cordoba is the Mezquita-Catedral, an architectural marvel that showcases the city's remarkable diversity. This structure is a vivid reflection of Cordoba's layered history, where each era has contributed to its present-day splendor. The Mezquita-Catedral was initially constructed as a mosque during the Islamic period, featuring a grand prayer hall adorned with iconic horseshoe arches and intricate red-and-white striped arches. The interplay of light and shadow, as it filters through these arches, creates an ethereal atmosphere that transports visitors to another time.

Within the heart of the Mezquita, an unexpected treasure awaits: a Christian cathedral that was integrated into the mosque. This architectural fusion encapsulates the intricate relationship between different faiths and their evolving significance over centuries. The juxtaposition of Moorish and Christian elements creates a mesmerizing blend of styles that speaks volumes about Cordoba's history of tolerance and coexistence.

Stepping out into the streets of Cordoba, you'll find yourself in the historic Jewish Quarter, known as the Judería. This enchanting neighborhood is a living canvas of cultural fusion, with narrow streets that wind past whitewashed buildings adorned with intricate ironwork and wooden balconies. Flower-filled patios and charming squares beckon you to explore every hidden corner. Among these charming alleys, the Calleja de las Flores stands out as a photogenic gem. Adorned with vibrant flowers and traditional Andalusian architecture, this alley captures the essence of Cordoba's visual allure. As you stroll through the Judería, the echoes of history reverberate through the stones, sharing tales of Jewish, Christian, and Moorish life that once intermingled here.

Cordoba's Alcázar de los Reyes Cristianos stands as both a fortress and a palace, an embodiment of the city's rich tapestry of stories. This architectural masterpiece has witnessed a plethora of historical events and has hosted various rulers throughout its existence. The palace's lush gardens, adorned with fragrant blossoms and meticulously manicured landscapes, offer a tranquil retreat from the bustle of the city. The tranquil ponds mirror the reflections of the palace's impressive towers, creating a serene and picturesque setting that allows you to immerse yourself in the rhythms of history.

In Cordoba, the past is not confined to museums or monuments; it's alive in every stone, every arch, and every corner of the city. Each step you take connects you to the footsteps of philosophers, scholars, artisans, and rulers who have contributed to Cordoba's multi-layered identity. The city beckons you to explore its rich tapestry of cultures, where every detail, whether it's an architectural flourish or a winding alley, tells a story.

In essence, Cordoba, along with Ronda and Granada, serves as a trinity of captivating destinations that offer a profound glimpse into the history, culture, and architectural wonders of Andalusia. Their unique charm lies in their ability to transport you through time, inviting you to immerse yourself in the echoes of a past that continues to resonate in the present. These cities stand as essential stops on any journey through the region, where the past and the present converge to create an unforgettable experience that enriches the soul and ignites the imagination.

CHAPTER TEN

PRACTICAL INFORMATION AND RESOURCES

10.1 Useful Travel Tips for a Smooth Visit

A successful trip to Malaga and the Costa del Sol hinges on careful planning and informed decision-making. To ensure your journey is as smooth as the Mediterranean breeze, consider the following travel tips:

Weather and Seasons: Enjoying the Mediterranean Climate

One of the primary draws of Malaga and the Costa del Sol is their remarkable Mediterranean climate. Characterized by mild, rainy winters and hot, dry summers, this climate sets the stage for a variety of outdoor activities and a year-round vibrant atmosphere.

Summers of Sunshine and Coastal Breezes

Summer, from June to August, is the peak tourist season. During these months, the region experiences its highest temperatures, with daily averages ranging from 25°C to 30°C (77°F to 86°F). The sun shines brightly, casting a golden hue on the sandy beaches and azure waters of the Mediterranean Sea. This is the perfect time to indulge in water sports, lounge on the sun-kissed shores, and bask in the vibrant energy of the coastal towns.

Embracing Shoulder Seasons: Spring and Fall

For travelers seeking a balance between comfortable temperatures and fewer crowds, the shoulder seasons of spring (April to May) and fall (September to October) offer an excellent compromise. During these months, temperatures hover between 15°C to 25°C (59°F to 77°F), creating a pleasant environment for exploration without the intense heat of summer.

Spring bursts forth with colorful blooms, and the landscape comes alive with the fragrant scent of flowers. Fall, on the other hand, paints the region in warm hues, making it a picturesque time for hiking in the surrounding mountains and exploring historic sites.

Respecting Local Customs: A Cultural Tapestry

Andalusian culture is a tapestry woven with warmth, hospitality, and time-honored traditions. When interacting with the locals, it's important to appreciate and engage with these customs, enhancing your experience and fostering positive connections.

Greeting and Etiquette

A simple smile and friendly greeting can go a long way in Andalusia. Locals often greet each other with a kiss on both cheeks or a warm handshake. Whether you're entering a shop, restaurant, or engaging in conversation, taking a moment to greet with genuine warmth will be reciprocated.

Appreciating Mealtime Traditions

Lunch and dinner times in Andalusia often differ from other countries. Lunch is typically served between 2:00 PM and

4:00 PM, while dinner starts around 9:00 PM or even later. This leisurely approach to meals reflects the region's emphasis on enjoying good food and company. Additionally, it's important to note that many businesses close for a siesta, or mid-afternoon break, usually from 2:00 PM to 5:00 PM.

Health and Safety: Navigating with Confidence

While the Costa del Sol is generally safe for travelers, it's always wise to exercise standard precautions to ensure a worry-free journey.

Personal Belongings and Security

Pickpocketing can occur in crowded tourist areas, so it's recommended to use a money belt or a secure bag for your valuables. Keep an eye on your belongings, especially in busy markets, public transportation, and other crowded spaces.

Nighttime Exploration

Malaga and its surrounding areas boast a lively nightlife, and it's generally safe to explore after dark. However, it's advisable to stay in well-lit and busy areas, especially if you're unfamiliar with the surroundings. If you're out late, consider using reputable transportation options like taxis to return to your accommodations.

Travel Insurance for Peace of Mind

Having comprehensive travel insurance is essential when visiting any destination. Ensure that your insurance covers medical emergencies, trip cancellations, and other unexpected situations. This precaution provides peace of mind, allowing you to focus on enjoying your journey without undue worry.

Safe Drinking Water: A Refreshing Assurance

The tap water in Malaga and the majority of the Costa del Sol is safe to drink. The region upholds high standards for water quality, making it suitable for consumption. If you have any reservations or a sensitive stomach, bottled water is widely available and offers an alternative option.

Navigating the Region: Public Transportation

Getting around Malaga and the Costa del Sol is both convenient and cost-effective, thanks to the efficient public transportation system.

Comprehensive Public Transport

Malaga boasts a well-connected network of buses and trains that facilitate easy travel within the city and to neighboring towns. The city's metro system, known as the Malaga Metro, is an excellent way to navigate the city center and beyond. These options offer a practical means of exploring the region's attractions without the hassle of driving and parking.

Consider Reloadable Transportation Cards

To streamline your travel experience, consider purchasing a reloadable transportation card. These cards provide access to various forms of public transportation and can be recharged as needed. Not only do they save you money on individual fares, but they also eliminate the need to purchase tickets for each journey.

In conclusion, navigating Malaga and the Costa del Sol requires an understanding of the climate, local customs, health and safety precautions, and transportation options. By embracing these elements, you'll be well-equipped to embark on an unforgettable journey through this enchanting region, immersing yourself in its natural beauty, rich culture, and warm hospitality.

10.2 Language, Currency, and Communication Essentials

Language: Bridging Cultural Connections

Spanish, specifically Castilian, is the official language of Spain. While English is commonly spoken in the tourism industry, taking the initiative to learn a few basic Spanish phrases can significantly enhance your travel experience and foster deeper connections with the locals.

Unlocking the Local Experience

Even a simple "hola" (hello) or "gracias" (thank you) can go a long way in breaking the ice and showing your appreciation for the culture. Learning how to order food, ask for directions, or engage in polite small talk allows you to immerse yourself in the daily rhythm of life in Malaga and the Costa del Sol.

Cultural Respect

Speaking a few words of the local language is a gesture of respect towards the culture and people of the region. Locals often appreciate the effort, and it can lead to more meaningful interactions, providing insights into their way of life and fostering a genuine exchange of experiences.

Currency: Navigating Financial Transactions

The Euro (EUR) is the official currency of Spain, and it's the accepted form of payment throughout Malaga and the Costa del Sol.

Currency Exchange Options

Currency exchange services are readily available in the region, with banks, exchange offices, and even some hotels offering these services. It's wise to compare rates and fees to ensure you're getting a fair deal when converting your money.

Card Payments and Cash Considerations

Credit and debit cards are widely accepted at most establishments, including restaurants, hotels, and shops. However, it's advisable to carry a moderate amount of cash, especially when visiting smaller local markets or cafes that might not have card payment facilities.

Emerging from the Digital Age: Communication

In the digital age, staying connected while traveling has become essential for various reasons, from navigation to sharing experiences with loved ones. Malaga and the Costa del Sol offer multiple ways to ensure you're well-connected during your visit.

Local SIM Cards and International Data Plans

If you're looking to stay connected through calls, texts, and data, consider purchasing a local SIM card upon arrival. These cards are available at convenience stores, mobile carrier shops, and even at the airport. Alternatively, you can activate an international data plan with your home provider before your trip.

Wi-Fi Availability

Free Wi-Fi is a common feature in many hotels, cafes, and public spaces throughout Malaga. Most accommodations offer Wi-Fi access to guests, and many restaurants and coffee shops also provide this service. This connectivity allows you to easily share your travel experiences, access maps, and stay in touch with friends and family.

Seamless Exploration

Understanding the local language, handling currency transactions, and staying connected digitally all contribute to a seamless and enriched exploration of Malaga and the Costa del Sol. By embracing these practical aspects, you can fully immerse yourself in the beauty, culture, and hospitality that the region has to offer.

CONCLUSION

Reflecting on Your Malaga and Costa del Sol Adventure

As you find yourself at the crossroads of your journey, where the captivating charms of Malaga and the Costa del Sol bid you farewell, it's an opportune time to gently step back and immerse yourself in the tapestry of memories you've woven. This chapter extends an invitation to you, the traveler, to temporarily detach from the whirlwind of activities and to relish in the beauty of reflection. Here, amid the pages of your travelogue, you have the chance to linger over the mosaic of experiences you've etched into your heart.

Allow the vivid vignettes of your exploration to resurface – from the sun-kissed beaches that warmed your spirit to the alleyways of Malaga's Old Town that whispered stories of ages past. Each experience, a brushstroke on the canvas of your journey, has contributed to the masterpiece you've painted during your time in this captivating corner of Spain.

In the midst of the quietude this chapter provides, take a mindful pause to savor the highlights that continue to dance in your memory. The architectural wonders, a testament to human creativity and craftsmanship, rise before your mind's eye once again. The intricate motifs of Moorish designs, the breathtaking Alhambra, and the modern marvels of Malaga beckon you to recall the awe they inspired.

As the aromas of tapas and paella waft through your recollection, let your taste buds remember the delightful culinary escapades you embarked upon. The vibrant flavors, the local delicacies, and the fusion of ingredients – all contribute to the symphony of tastes that is an integral part of your journey.

Gently close your eyes and transport yourself back to the sun-soaked shores that cradle the azure waters of the Mediterranean Sea. The sensation of golden sand between your toes, the rhythmic sound of waves, and the caress of the sea breeze – these sensations encapsulate the essence of your time on the Costa del Sol.

Embracing the Allure of Malaga and the Costa del Sol: Begin by revisiting the origins of your intrigue that led you to this exquisite region. Allow the memories of your prelude – the whispers of Picasso's legacy, the intrigue of vibrant festivals awaiting your arrival, and the tranquility that comes with lounging beside the expansive Mediterranean – to come to the forefront. These were the promises that lured you in, and now, they are the realities you hold dear.

A Brief Overview of Your Journey: In the quiet confines of reflection, unfurl the parchment of your journey and let its panoramic tapestry unfold before you. Trace the trajectory of your footsteps, from the cobbled lanes of Malaga's historic core that echoed with history, to the sprawling landscapes of the Costa del Sol that invited adventure. Within these recollections lie the encounters with kindred souls, the laughter exchanged with locals, and the nuances that animated each locale.

Let this chapter stand as a tribute to the experiences you've harvested, a pause in time that allows you to contemplate not just where you've ventured, but the soulful voyage you've undertaken. So as the chapter turns and you navigate the final chapters of your Malaga and Costa del Sol escapade, remember that this reflection is a tapestry woven by you, and its threads are the vivacious hues of the memories you now carry with you.

Fond Memories and Inspirations for Future Journeys

As you wrap up your adventure in Malaga and the Costa del Sol, it's important to consider the lasting impact this journey will have on your future travels. The memories and inspirations you've gained from this experience will serve as valuable resources for your future explorations. This chapter encourages you to channel the spirit of your adventure into planning and dreaming about your next destinations.

Cherishing Fond Memories: Take a moment to recount your favorite memories and moments from your time in Malaga and the Costa del Sol. Whether it's a mesmerizing sunset over the Mediterranean, a lively flamenco performance, or a particularly delicious tapas dish, these memories will always hold a special place in your heart.

Lessons from the Journey: Reflect on the lessons you've learned during your travels. Perhaps you've gained insights into the local culture, discovered the importance of embracing spontaneity, or developed new skills through adventurous activities. Consider how these lessons can enrich your future journeys.

Fueling Wanderlust: Use the inspiration you've gained from your Malaga and Costa del Sol adventure to fuel your passion for travel. Explore possibilities for your next destinations, and allow the experiences you've had to shape your future travel plans.

Sharing Your Story: Your journey is not just yours alone. Share your experiences and stories with friends, family, and fellow travelers. Your insights and recommendations can inspire others to embark on their own explorations of this captivating region.

As you reflect on your adventure in Malaga and the Costa del Sol and gather your fond memories and inspirations for future journeys, remember that the experiences you've had will continue to enrich your life long after you've returned home.

Printed in Great Britain
by Amazon